OPERATION *BARBAROSSA*

OPERATION

BARBAROSSA

Nazi Germany's War in the East,
1941–1945

CHRISTIAN HARTMANN

OXFORD
UNIVERSITY PRESS

OXFORD
UNIVERSITY PRESS

Great Clarendon Street, Oxford, OX2 6DP,
United Kingdom

Oxford University Press is a department of the University of Oxford.
It furthers the University's objective of excellence in research, scholarship,
and education by publishing worldwide. Oxford is a registered trade mark of
Oxford University Press in the UK and in certain other countries

Originally published as *Unternehmen Barbarossa:
Der Deutsche Krieg im Osten, 1941–1945*
© Verlag C. H. Beck oHG, München 2011
Author: Christian Hartmann

The moral rights of the author have been asserted

First published in English 2013

Impression: 1

British Library Cataloguing in Publication Data
Data available

ISBN 978–0–19–966078–0

Printed in Great Britain by
Clays Ltd, St Ives plc

Links to third party websites are provided by Oxford in good faith and
for information only. Oxford disclaims any responsibility for the materials
contained in any third party website referenced in this work.

CONTENTS

CONTENTS

LIST OF MAPS

LIST OF FIGURE AND ILLUSTRATIONS

Figure

Illustrations

PUBLISHER'S ACKNOWLEDGEMENT

The publishers would like to extend their especial thanks to Professor Jonathan Wright for his editorial contribution to the preparation of the English edition of this book.

The real war will never get in the books.

Walt Whitman (1819–92)

1

Introduction

Never before or since had there been a war like this one. A war that cost so much blood, with such enormous repercussions, or that etched itself so deeply into the collective memory of its contemporaries as the war that raged between the German Reich and the Soviet Union from 1941 to 1945. History is not short of conflicts both bloody and momentous in their consequences that have seared themselves into the memory of posterity, but there are not many, even among the pivotal conflicts of world history, that are comparable to the German–Soviet War. Everything about it was gargantuan—the numbers deployed, the theatre over which it was fought, and, not least, the numbers of victims that it claimed.

It was a conflict for which it is difficult to name an equivalent, in either its scale or its consequences. The Allied victory in the Second World War obviously stemmed from a variety of causes, and it would naturally be misleading to reduce explanations for the defeat of Hitler's Germany to a mere handful of factors and events. But it is undeniable that the Soviet Union played a large part, if not the largest part, in that victory. It was there that the

Wehrmacht bled itself dry, and it was in the East that it first became apparent that Hitler's deluded and criminal attempt at National Socialist world domination would end in failure. The reverberations were so immense that they continued long after 1945; Operation *Barbarossa* fundamentally changed the map of Europe. Without it, the ethnic reorganization and Sovietization of its eastern half would have been unimaginable. But, above all, it was the 'Great Patriotic War' and its millions of dead that turned the Soviet Union into a superpower.

Finally, the way the war was fought was itself extraordinary. It was a fight for existence between the twentieth century's two great totalitarian movements—and the conduct of both sides was correspondingly extreme. Both Nazi Germany and the Stalinist Soviet Union fought the war as though it were a crusade. The result was an orgy of violence, even if much of the fighting at the front as often as not was of a conventional nature. What was crucial, however, was that a new type of war developed, an increasingly ideological, total war, one that returned almost to its atavistic origins. Moreover, this was neither a peripheral colonial war, nor a civil war fought according to its own set of rules and conventions. It was a pivotal conflict fought between two of Europe's most cultured and venerable nations. The effects of the new way in which the belligerents looked at both themselves and each other are not to be underestimated. Since 1945, there have been ever more examples of the extent to which modern warfare is characterized by what are generally acknowledged as war crimes—and of the way such crimes have to a degree even come to replace it. It was during the German–Soviet War that much of this behaviour became common practice once more.

And this was no accident—the German leadership wanted it that way. Operation *Barbarossa* was a war of aggression that the Third Reich started out of choice not necessity. It was also—something that would prove even more calamitous—conceived from the very first as an ideological war of ethnic annihilation. That is not so say that the Soviet Union, whose leaders had embarked on the adventure of the Hitler–Stalin Pact in 1939, was completely blameless in radicalizing the way in which the war was waged. It, too, was a totalitarian and deeply criminal regime, and became all the more so when it found itself with its back to the wall. But it remains indisputable that the initiative for the war came from Germany and that, seen as a whole, the German atrocities during the war weigh significantly more heavily than do the Soviet ones.

These experiences inevitably left a deep impression on the societies that were involved. Even today there are few things as important to the national identity of the post-Soviet nations as the memory of victory over Hitler's Germany. The losers, on the other hand, have distanced themselves fundamentally from the ideas and institutions that made such a war possible. This is not just because the invasion ended in such complete disaster for the invaders. An even greater burden in the long term was the slowly emerging German realization that they had not only sacrificed in vain, but had also fought for something that was so thoroughly evil.

The memory of Operation *Barbarossa* is sure to outlive those who witnessed it. To say this is merely to give an inkling of the forces that it unleashed. But how do we explain it? And why did it even happen in the first place?

2

Politics 1940–1941

Europe in July 1940

The Second World War seemed to have been decided early—not in May 1945, but after less than a year, in June 1940. A quick glance at the map of Europe would have been enough to suggest that this was the case. The German *Wehrmacht* had literally overrun its opponents—Poland (1 September to 16 October 1939), then Norway and Denmark (9 April to 10 June 1940), and finally France and the Low Countries (10 May to 22 June 1940). Poland and Scandinavia had essentially been a warm-up, but that hardly applied to the German offensive in the West. After the shockingly rapid victory over the combined armies of France, Belgium, and the Netherlands as well as the British Expeditionary Force, the end of the war seemed close at hand. France, the 'hereditary enemy' and predominant German fear in the First World War, was conquered and occupied, the British driven back onto their islands. Although it had saved the greater part of its ground forces, at least the soldiers, and had at its disposal one of the world's strongest navies, a modern air force, and the almost inexhaustible resources of the

4

Commonwealth, the island kingdom was politically isolated for the time being. In summer 1940, Britain was the only one of Hitler's opponents left, and it appeared to be reeling, militarily as well as psychologically. Otherwise, the European continent itself was almost entirely under German control.

No one had expected this, particularly not in such a short time. Almost precisely twenty-one years previously, on 28 June 1919, Germany seemed to have lost everything and not just the First World War. In the Treaty of Versailles, Germany was forced to admit its sole responsibility for that war (Article 231) and therefore to foot the bill. It was high: loss of around 13 per cent of its territory, reparations to the value of 138 billion Goldmarks (at their value on 21 April 1921), surrender of all colonies and the majority of its merchant fleet, reduction of its Armed Forces to 115,000 men, and much more besides. The Allied conditions were stringent, petty, and directed at a society that in the previous years had lost over two million soldiers and a million civilians to war, hunger, and sickness. However, the 'Versailles Diktat'—this was the note struck in Germany at the time—did not actually imperil the existence of the German nation, and that was the real problem. The Allied victors had neither destroyed the German Reich nor really made peace with it nor dared to attempt a new beginning with its Weimar leaders. They had instead struck a fateful and dangerous middle way: they had weakened the Reich, humiliated it, and provoked in German society a mindset characterized by deep resentment of the victorious Western powers, by fear of worse, by an emotional hostility to modern civilization, by a widespread longing for 'national rebirth', and, ultimately, for revenge. On a basic level, those longings were not nearly as impossible to achieve as they seemed. Austria–Hungary, one of the other great losers in the First World War, had disintegrated into individual states, and unification of German Austria with the German Reich, the long-discussed 'Greater German solution' to the question of how the Germans were to be politically organized, finally seemed possible. Though that, too, was expressly forbidden by the Treaty of Versailles, at least for the time being.

Another loser in the First World War had been Russia, even though it had fought on the Allied side. It left the war through the Treaty of Brest-Litovsk (3 March 1918) because a bloody civil war had paralysed the country after the February and October revolutions of 1917. Alongside a number of significant differences, there was also a series of striking parallels between the situations of the two empires, the German and the Russian. Both were former great powers that the First World War had left weak, traumatized, and dismantled; both had forms of government that were entirely new to them, and both were totally isolated in international politics. It was no coincidence that these two outcasts found their way to each other in the Treaty of Rapallo (16 April 1922). And there was another parallel that first became visible later, after 1933. The military, political, and economic crises had radicalized both Russian and German society to an unprecedented extent, albeit in almost opposite ideological directions. Despite the differences, these two mutually hostile ways of looking at the world had in common that they both offered a future and a salvation, one for race and nation, the other for all humanity. It can in some ways be seen as an anti-thetical relationship, a tension between right and left that would leave its mark on the interwar period. After 1933, Nazi Germany and the Soviet Union made no secret of their deep enmity. But, despite that, a war of anything more than propaganda at first seemed highly unlikely. Between the Soviet Union and Germany lay the 'cordon sanitaire', that world of central European states called into existence after the First World War. The other, more important point was that neither was then militarily or politically anywhere near being able to wage such a war.

The strategic possibilities available to Nazi Germany in 1933 were, in fact, very modest. The horizons of German foreign policy extended only as far as the borders of the Weimar Republic, and its aims were confined to revising the Versailles Peace Treaty, to such ambitions as reuniting the Saarland with the rest of Germany (January 1935), and having the *Wehrmacht* reoccupy the demilitarized Rhineland (March 1936). These were no more than territorial adjustments within the German sphere of power. That changed in 1938. With the untroubled *Anschluss* of Austria in March and the rather more dramatic annexation of the Sudetenland in October, Nazi Germany was able to expand its territory for the first time. Both could be justified by the principle of a people's right to self-determination, as championed by the American President Woodrow Wilson at the end of the First World War. Soon afterwards, however, in March 1939, Hitler demonstrated that he was not thinking of the borders and traditions of Bismarck's Germany when he occupied the so-called rump Czechoslovakia, now administered as the Protectorate of Bohemia and Moravia. This was brutal annexation, and it was also a historical turning point, because now at last the Western powers had to recognize that their politics of soothing and compromise, of 'Appeasement', had failed. Hitler simply ignored the guarantees they made to East European states. When he then tried to cow Poland politically and territorially, he left Britain and France with no choice. The German invasion of Poland on 1 September 1939 was followed two days later by the British and French declarations of war. With that the

German Reich had begun something for which its *Führer* had long planned and prepared—the appropriation of *Lebensraum* (living space) by means of war.

In July 1940, this first European stage seemed almost complete. If, however, the map of German conquests up to this date is examined more closely, it rapidly becomes clear how heterogeneous the German power block really was. There were areas occupied by German troops, completely or in part (Bohemia and Moravia, Poland, Denmark, Norway, Belgium, the Netherlands, Luxembourg, and France), there were allies (the Soviet Union, Italy, Romania, and Hungary after November 1940, Bulgaria after March 1941), friends (Finland, Romania, Spain), and largely dependent states (Slovakia), while the number of neutral powers shrank continually in the period up to summer 1941. After the Balkan campaign and the German–Italian occupation of Yugoslavia and Greece (6 April to 23 April 1941), only a few islands of Europe were spared war and dictatorship: Switzerland, Sweden, Ireland, Portugal, and Turkey, and even they were exposed to the mounting pressure of German foreign politics.

At that point, Nazi Germany had almost all of Europe within its reach, and its military and economic potential was correspondingly large. Opposition hardly existed. Britain's offensive capabilities were exhausted for the time being, and the European resistance movements were yet to organize themselves. The attitude of the occupied European states was mostly one of *l'attentisme*, a careful wait-and-see. For Hitler and his followers, this was the most advantageous position conceivable. In summer 1940, he stood at the zenith of his power, and almost everything seemed to indicate that the enormous risk of starting a war had indeed paid off.

Hitler's ideology and strategy

There are many accounts of how German power came to extend itself so suddenly across Europe—political and military ones, social or historical, and each of them is accurate in its own way. The single most important impulse, however, and that by some distance, came from an individual, Adolf Hitler (1889–1945). Understanding him as the real motor of this development does not mean falling into the trap of biographical reductiveness. Of course, there were many supra-personal tendencies, resentments, and longings bound up in Hitler's character, and, without the obedient or enthusiastic mass of 'national comrades', his thinking would naturally not have had much of an effect on the rest of Europe. But it is also true that by summer 1940 Hitler had manœuvred himself into a situation in which he, as unchallenged Commander-in-Chief, was as free as he never was before or afterwards to draw the plans for his dream of a great and mighty empire. His power and the opportunities open to him were in every sense tremendous, and correspondingly tremendous was the influence that he as an individual was able to exercise over world politics.

Rarely was this as evident as it was in Operation *Barbarossa*. He had laid the tracks, he alone and in secret, in the well-guarded and prohibited areas of the *Führer* headquarters and residences. Here there were plenty of ideologues, functionaries, or bureaucrats who accepted his decisions, praised them, or even supported them enthusiastically. But how were things seen by the other, 'normal' Germans? Whether they, without their *Führer*, would ever have fallen in for an attack on the Soviet Union is a speculative question, but surely no idle one. Naturally, the ideological potential that was then discharged in the war against the Soviet

Union—anti-Bolshevism, anti-Semitism, anti-Slavism, and also a naked imperialism—had all been widespread, though far from uniform, in German society up to summer 1940. But it is entirely questionable whether this ideological saturation would have sufficed for the Germans to plunge themselves like so many lemmings into this homicidal and ultimately suicidal undertaking. Many soldiers certainly had misgivings about it, and when they were informed of the plan decided upon by their Commander-in-Chief a few hours before the assault in the night between 21 and 22 June, they could have guessed that the campaign would be bloody, hard, and ruinous. In the long weeks and months beforehand, they had been transported to the eastern borders of the German empire without having been given even a rough idea of what they were there to do. The official line was that this was a dummy deployment intended to divert attention from the real plan, a seaborne invasion of Great Britain. They knew no more than that, because the decisions about this war, about its goals and the manner in which it would be fought, were all to be made by Hitler.

That is not to say that his decision-making process was not also subject to external pressures. In summer 1940, there were three considerations that were most dangerous for him: Great Britain, the Commonwealth, and Winston Churchill (1874–1965). Churchill had become Prime Minister on 10 May 1940, the day of the German invasion of the West, and it was—in Joachim Fest's masterly formulation—'as though Europe, entangled in the complicity of its agreements with Hitler and deeply defeatist in mood, rediscovered in this man its norms, its language and its will to self-assertion'. Churchill had recognized more quickly and clearly than many of his contemporaries that Nazism not only threatened his country or his continent, but fundamentally threatened the entire contemporary world order. And, like hardly any other statesman before him, Churchill was ready and able to set himself against the apparently invincible German conquerors using all available means, even when that meant placing the entire British Empire on the scales. Above all, it was Churchill's will to resist and the readiness of British society to pursue his policy of 'victory at all costs' that drew the line against which the insatiable German lust for conquest finally foundered. Internationally it was a lonely policy, made without the support of any real allies. In his memoirs, Churchill reduced the title of what would presumably be the decisive chapter of the Second World War to a single word: Alone. It truly was 'the finest hour', and not only for Churchill.

For his German counterpart, this immediately presented a range of concerns, both of power politics and of political ideology. Hitler had always hoped for an alliance between Germany and Great Britain in which the congenial 'Germanic' partners would share world domination by land and sea. But even before 1939, he had eventually to accept that these ideas found only few friends in the British Isles. Equally ineffectual was Hitler's 'appeal for peace' with Great Britain (19 July 1940), and so his understanding of the world left him no other choice but to force this equally hated and admired naval power to surrender. But how? The three approaches that the German strategists adopted in the subsequent weeks—an intensified air war against the British Isles as prelude to their invasion, a comprehensive U-boat war against the British convoys in the Atlantic, and, finally, an intensifying engagement around the Mediterranean—all remained inconclusive. Despite all sacrifices and efforts made up to the end of the year 1940, nothing essential changed in the strategic stalemate of Europe. The initiative was still Germany's. The overwhelming reserves of the Commonwealth, however, combined with, in the long term, those of the USA, indicated that time was not on Germany's side.

Hitler was not prepared to draw any political conclusions from that knowledge. Instead of limiting or ending the war, he wanted to widen it. What he began to tinker with from autumn 1940 onwards, albeit with some hesitation, was not the content but merely the order of his plans. Why not realize his final political goal, the great war of conquest in the East, immediately? Why not decide one stagnating war by means of another? Hitler was well aware that such a radical shift of emphasis in German strategy would present incalculable risks. Until then, the Soviet Union had proved itself a reliable ally and provider of raw materials. Not only that, it covered his back against the danger of a war on two fronts, something by which the German Reich had already been broken in the First World War. But was it not possible that this knot could be chopped with a single blow? What tempted Hitler more and more was the idea of a global blitzkrieg in which each war would nourish the next. If one 'ever really tackles' a colossus like the Soviet Union, Hitler revealed to his military advisers, 'it breaks apart far more quickly than the world would have guessed'. With the help of its new 'Eastern zone'—this was Hitler's vision— Germany would conquer everyone, first Great Britain and then ultimately the USA. It was, as it was called afterwards, a step-by-step plan, each step a step towards German world domination.

At first these were just exercises on the map, naturally top secret. But they soon sufficed to cool relations with the Soviet Union. When foreign minister Vyacheslav Molotov, visiting Berlin for the first time on 12 and 13 November 1940, made matters worse by describing the USSR's territorial intentions in Europe—they aimed above all at securing Soviet influence in Scandinavia, the southern Balkans, and the Turkish straits—Hitler understood this as a conclusive signal. His hesitation ended. As soon afterwards as 5 December 1940, he informed his military advisers that the struggle for 'European hegemony' would be decided 'in the fight against the Soviet Union'. Thirteen days later, he signed his famous directive no. 21. Its first sentence read: 'The German Wehrmacht must be prepared to crush Soviet Russia in a quick campaign even before the end of the war against England.'

The monstrous scheme: a Greater Germanic empire

Hitler's decision to invade the Soviet Union was not solely the result of power politics. His motives were more complex and had a far longer back story. He had wanted this war for a long time and in it he saw the chance totally to annihilate the mortal enemies of Nazism: Bolsheviks, Jews, and Slavs. In this Hitler was returning to his political origins, to the boundless phantasmagorias that he measured, not against the art of the possible, but against the principles of the exorbitant fantasy world he had designed around himself: 'We will stop the endless Germanic migrations towards the south and west of Europe and instead turn our gaze to the land in the east. We will finally leave behind the colonial and mercantile politics of the pre-war era and move on to the territorial politics of the future.'

This extract from Hitler's statement of faith, *Mein Kampf*, demonstrates how early he set his sights on this target. In his politics, however, it had been only vaguely recognizable since then. It was

ILLUSTRATION 1. In military commander mode: Hitler and Mussolini on a visit to the Eastern Front, 26 August 1941

in 1938–9 that his intentions became more distinct. Until that point, the success of Hitler's politics had, after all, been due in large part to letting tactical compromise blur the absolute quality of his ideology and thus bring it into the realm of the practical.

But, from now on, utopias and doctrines would carry the day unhindered.

Its aim was not only annihilation. Because Hitler considered 'the East' to be 'waste and empty', he wanted to shape it as he saw fit— without any regard either for its past or for the people who were actually living there. It was there that he saw the future of the Germans or indeed the entire 'Germanic race'. It was as though a malicious child were reorganizing the world: peoples were transplanted, destroyed, resettled, 'nordicized', or classified as 'slave races', all with complete contempt for whatever cultures or nations that had developed in those territories. Even the history of the twentieth century witnessed hardly anything comparable. What is characteristic of the atmosphere in Nazi Germany is that the *Führer* did not remain alone in all of this. Though these top-secret war games were initially presented only within the circle of power drawn close around the Reich's headquarters, there were more than enough 'specialists' willing to accommodate themselves to Hitler's ideas or indeed, with horribly apparent eagerness, transform his lunatic schemes into concrete government policy. This was the work less of his entourage than—what is worse—of real professionals: the traditional ministerial bureaucracy, party functionaries, officers of the General Staff, scholars, diplomats, and also some industrialists. On these planners' maps of the future, the 'Greater Germanic empire of the German Nation' would eventually come to stretch from the Atlantic coast all the way to the western foothills of the Urals. Its core would be the Greater German Reich, extended westwards to include significant parts of France and eastwards to swallow Bohemia, Moravia, and all of Poland. The model structure of this empire, however, was to consist not of the vassal states in the West or the Balkans, but of 'Reich Commissariats'—enormous swathes

MAP 1. Utopia. The 'Greater Germanic Reich of the German Nation'

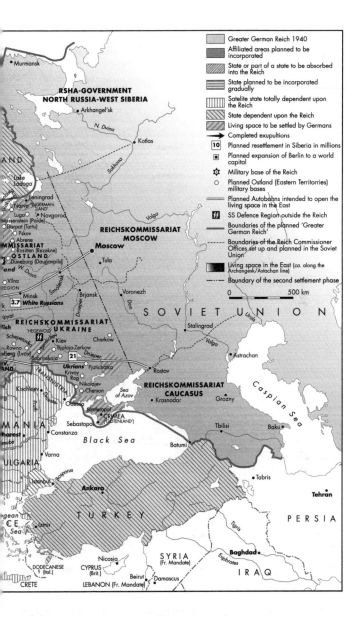

Legend:

Greater German Reich 1940

Affiliated areas planned to be incorporated

State or part of a state to be absorbed into the Reich

State planned to be incorporated gradually

Satellite state totally dependent upon the Reich

State dependent upon the Reich

Living space to be settled by Germans

→ Completed expultions

[10] Planned resettlement in Siberia in millions

■ Planned expansion of Berlin to a world capital

✿ Military base of the Reich

○ Planned Ostland (Eastern Territorries) military bases

Planned Autobahns intended to open the living space in the East

SS Defence Region outside the Reich

Boundaries of the planned 'Greater German Reich'

Boundaries of the Reich Commissioner Offices set up and planned in the Soviet Union

Living space in the East (ca. along the Archangesk/Astachan line)

Boundary of the second settlement phase

0   500 km

Map labels:

Murmansk

RSHA-GOVERNMENT
NORTH RUSSIA-WEST SIBERIA

Arkhangel'sk

N. Dvina

Kotlas

Suchona

AND

Lake Ladoga

Leningrad

Norva   INGERMAN-LAND

Lugo   Novgorod

Weissenstein (Paide)

Dorpat (Tartu)

Pskov

Abrene

MMISSARIAT   Rositten (Rezekne)

OSTLAND

Düneburg (Daugavpils)

and   W. Dvina

Volga

REICHSKOMMISSARIAT
MOSCOW

Moscow

Tula

Vilna
REGION

Minsk   Smolensk

3.7 White Russians   Brjansk   Voronezh

ipyat   Dnieper

Don

REICHSKOMMISSARIAT
UKRAINE

'HEGEWOLD'

Schepetovka   Kiev   Charkow

Rowno   Bjalaja-Zerkow

berg (Lvov)   Babrinskaja   Dnieper

S O V I E T   U N I O N

Stalingrad

Volga   Astrachan

Ukrians   Pjatichatka

Krivoy Rog   Rostov

Nikolajev

Kischinev   Cherson

Odessa   Sea of Azov

Simferopol   REICHSKOMMISSARIAT
CAUCASUS

CRIMEA ('GOTENLAND')   Krasnodar   Grozny

Sebastopol

MANIA   Tbilisi   Baku

harest   Black   Sea   Batumi

Constanza

ULGARIA   Varna

C a s p i a n   S e a

Istanbul   Bosporus   Tabris

Ankara   Tehran

gean   CE   Izmir   T U R K E Y   P E R S I A

Sea

Tigris

Nicosia   Baghdad

DODECANESE (Ital.)   SYRIA (Fr. Mandate)

CYPRUS (Brit.)   Beirut   Damascus   Euphrates   I R A Q

CRETE   LEBANON (Fr. Mandate)

of Scandinavia and, especially, of the East: the Ukraine, 'Eastland' (Belarus and the Baltic states), Moscow, and the Caucasus.

What this meant for the people living there could be read in the General Plan East. Commissioned in 1940 by the head of the SS, Heinrich Himmler, this plan provided the political blueprint for the subsequent German occupation of Eastern Europe. Thirty-one million Slavs, possibly also fifty-one million (the German planners were generous) Poles, Byelorussians, Ukrainians, and Czechs, were to be driven into Siberia, where they would either be left to their fate or 'scrapped' at once. Only those 'capable of Germanization' and potential slave labourers would be left. Himmler had already let it be known that these 'alien races' would have to learn 'that it is a divine commandment to be obedient to the Germans, as well as honest, hard-working and well-behaved'. They were to serve the occupiers, some five to twelve million 'Germanic settlers', who were to be recruited both within the Reich and around the rest of Europe. With the help of a giant system of thirty-nine large 'defence settlements' and countless 'defence villages' connected to each other by motorways and railways, they were to rule a country that would be shielded from the lands to the East by an enormous wall.

As deranged and amoral as these atrocious plans may seem, they really did form the basis of German politics. If they were never or only incompletely realized, that was by no means because the German leadership did not take them seriously. The problem was rather that the war they initiated developed in a direction quite unlike the one they had originally expected. This presents a central problem in the history of National Socialism. Here historians are dealing with a utopian project whose conversion into reality was stifled in its nascent phase, so much so that in retrospect it is often difficult to make out its true ambitions. Its architects also worked hard after 1945 to play down the extreme nature and inhumanity of their intentions. But it was precisely this plan that was the primary motivation for Operation *Barbarossa*. That the behaviour of the Germans altered under the influence of the war and that there was subsequently a division of responsibilities among the aggressors are matters that belong to a later history. Most important at the outbreak of war were ideology and politics; the well-known maxim that war is only the continuation of politics by other means has seldom seemed so justified as it was in the case of Operation *Barbarossa*.

Stalin's ideology and strategy

Did the Soviet leadership—did, above all, the Soviet dictator Joseph V. Stalin (1878–1953)—have an inkling of what was being prepared in the West? Yes and no. Naturally, the deployment of a million-strong army on the borders of the Soviet Union (and the careful sounding-out by German diplomats of potential allies in an Eastern campaign) could not be kept entirely secret. Up to 22 June 1941, the warnings came time and again. Despite that and despite the ever more numerous indications of a German invasion, Stalin remained dogmatically fixed on the course that he had already set for his foreign policy, a course at that point oriented primarily towards the Non-Aggression Pact with Germany. How do we explain this?

The Soviet Union's foreign policy had been confronted with an unusual conceptual problem from the moment of its birth. The Bolsheviks had decided the Revolution and Civil War (1917–21) in their own favour, but their hope of a global revolution had not

ILLUSTRATION 2. Friends? Signing the Nazi–Soviet Non-Aggression pact in Moscow. First from the right is Molotov, Stalin is third from the right, and fifth from the right is Ribbentrop.

been realized. The USSR had remained the only socialist state—sovereign, vast, and with tremendous ideological aims, but weak in influence and isolated from a world that reacted with suspicion and often indeed with outright hostility to this political experiment. In the light of the revolutionary future that the Bolsheviks preached to all other countries, that was not entirely unjustified.

In reality, however, the world revolution was gradually becoming mere rhetoric. Since the end of the 1920s and the consolidation of Stalin's unconditional dictatorship, Soviet foreign policy had begun to alter its approach. The principle of 'socialism in one country' increasingly came to shape the external politics of the Soviet Union. In practical terms, that meant a readoption of power politics in the traditional style and a careful return from international isolation, partly in order—in the Soviet formulation—to loosen the 'encirclement by imperialist powers'. This began through close cooperation with Germany (Treaty of Rapallo, 16 April 1922; Treaty of Berlin, 24 April 1926) and continued in a series of non-aggression pacts with such close neighbours as Turkey (1925), Persia (1927), and Afghanistan (1931), as well as with Finland, Latvia, Estonia, and Poland in 1932. Not long after seizing power, however, in September 1933, Hitler had let it be known internally that the current 'German–Russian relations [were] objectively not sustainable in the long term'. With the signing of the German–Polish non-aggression pact of January 1934, at the very latest, Soviet foreign policy found itself having to adjust. Its new basis was provided by two mutual assistance pacts, with France (2 May 1935) and Czechoslovakia (16 May 1935). This system of collective security was enabled by the Soviet Union's having joined the League of Nations in September 1934 (a year before the exit of Germany and Japan) and by the new strategy of the popular front, which the Comintern, the Communist International in Moscow, announced to the world in 1935.

But how viable was this system really? In the harsh reality of international politics, the Soviet Union remained an outsider. It was unable to do more than react to the political situation that the other powers created. Could its security really be guaranteed with treaties and resolutions? The Sudetenland crisis in autumn 1938 seemed only to justify once again Stalin's almost pathological distrust of the hated capitalist countries. The Western powers had caved in to Hitler, and the Soviet Union, by contrast, had not even been asked to participate in the solution of this international dispute. Was the Soviet Union, after everything, not once again threatened with encirclement by the capitalist states? Would it perhaps even use fascist Germany as a spearhead against the first and only socialist country? That he himself did not make the slightest attempt to rescue his Czechoslovak allies was something that the Soviet dictator studiously failed to notice. What determined his thinking was the belief that the Western powers wanted to embroil his country in a war with Germany, something he soon stated publicly, at the 18th CPSU party conference in March 1939. It was true that, in spring 1939, the international situation was becoming ever more tense; when and between whom the imminent war would break out, however, was something that still remained undetermined. Stalin's nervousness and fear of betrayal were closely mirrored by the mental state of the crisis's actual instigator, Hitler. It was becoming increasingly apparent to him how isolated Germany would be after its invasion of Poland, something that had been set in stone long ago. Although he and the Italian dictator Benito Mussolini had signed the so-called Pact of Steel amid a great propaganda fanfare on 22 May 1939, German doubts about this alliance were confirmed soon after the outbreak of war in September. Fascist Italy first declared itself 'non-combatant' and decided to join the German side only on 10 June 1940, when the war against France was already as good as over.

But on whom could the German strategists really rely at that point? The only man who might be an answer to that question was Stalin, who, for his part, had in the preceding years never completely ruled out the possibility of an alliance with Germany. Although the ideological contrasts could hardly be starker and although the two tyrants' strategic intentions were entirely contradictory, their short-term interests seemed to complement each other rather well. Hitler wanted his rear secure, at least initially, and Stalin wanted to keep his country out of a general European war, for the time being. After all the twists and turns of international diplomacy, the result, on 23 August 1939, was the Nazi–Soviet Non-Aggression Pact, which immediately turned European politics on its head. The absolutely secret additional protocol, which explicitly and brutally divided Eastern Europe between the two dictatorships, corresponded to one of Stalin's other goals. He wanted to use the opportunities afforded him by the crisis to make territorial gains and so take up in more or less disguised fashion the old hegemonic endeavours of the Tsarist regime, all the while keeping the Soviet Union out of the war. 'The war will be fought between two groups of capitalist states,' Stalin explained in the Kremlin at the start of September 1939. 'We have nothing against it if they batter and weaken each other. It would be no bad thing if Germany were to knock the richest capitalist countries (particularly England) off their feet.'

This plan seemed to be working. As expected, a war broke out between Germany and the Western powers, initially disabling both sides. Meanwhile, the Soviet Union was able to extend its borders westwards bit by bit with no risk of involvement in a truly dangerous conflict. In quick succession Soviet troops occupied eastern Poland (17 September to 6 October 1939), then the three Baltic states (15 and 17 June 1940), and finally the eastern part of Romania—that is, Bessarabia and the northern Bukovina (28 June to 1 July 1940). In the winter campaign against Finland (30 November 1939 to 12 March 1940) the Soviet Union was also eventually able to 'retrieve' the south-eastern part of the country (West Karelia).

It was not only this territorial booty; the shockingly rapid German successes also gave Stalin a good reason not to rock the boat when it came to his powerful ally in the West. That was also the motive for extending the cooperation between the two arch-enemies of yesterday into other areas. On 28 September 1939 came a Boundary and Friendship Treaty, followed, on 11 February 1940 and 10 January 1941, by economic and trade agreements. The enormous supplies delivered by the Soviet Union to the German Reich (in 1940–1 their total value reached more than 618 million Reichsmark, against German goods to the value of 532 million Reichsmark) were indispensable to the latter's war effort. Right up until the last moment, the Soviet goods trains were still rolling into the West. In effect, that meant that, without Soviet oil, the German panzers would hardly have managed to reach the outskirts of Moscow.

Militarily, too, the Soviet side tried to avoid provocation wherever possible. The officers of the German General Staff recognized quite clearly that there were 'no indications of Russian activity directed against us', and, in September 1940, the State Secretary of the Foreign Office, Ernst Freiherr von Weizsäcker, was of the opinion that 'there is no reason to fear that the Russians will attack us'. It is quite evident that the German leadership did not really feel threatened by the Red Army at that point; as an opponent, it was hardly to be taken seriously. There is, therefore, not the remotest justification for the claims made subsequently, that in Operation *Barbarossa* the *Wehrmacht* had been carrying out a pre-emptive strike so as to anticipate an imminent Soviet invasion. That is not to suggest that Stalin did not pursue imperialist goals that aimed partly at the centre of Europe. They were, however, to be realized *later*, once capitalist Europe had exhausted itself in a new world war. Only then would the Soviet Union 'appear at the last, to throw the decisive weight onto the scales'. That was something Stalin had announced as early as 1925, just at the same point in time when his German antithesis was publishing the first volume of his credo, *Mein Kampf*.

3

The Eve of War

The invaders

While Stalin continued to place his faith in the complex mechanisms of his foreign–political axioms, the German preparations rolled on undisturbed. By June 1941, the Wehrmacht's leaders had gathered 3.3 million soldiers on the borders with the Soviet Union. The total number of German soldiers deployed during the course of the war in the East is estimated at around ten million. In other words, it was the largest military force Germany had ever assembled. But it would not be large enough.

The explanation for this is simple. The economic and demographic resources available within the German area of control were simply too small for a war on multiple fronts against a coalition as strong as the Allies. But can the course of a war really be explained with only a handful of statistical comparisons? Military reality is often far more complex. Suffice it to mention only the German campaign in the West and that, in the Soviet Union, too, the *Wehrmacht* was initially triumphant. Why was that?

The majority of the German soldiers believed that the war was for a good cause, at least at first. They were also experienced, hardened, reasonably solidly equipped, well trained, and excellently led at the tactical level; benefiting also from the element of surprise made their initial success secure. These soldiers were used to fighting a land war, something that applied equally to most members of the Luftwaffe, which made up 27 per cent of the invasion force. By contrast, the German Navy was never more than peripheral to the Eastern campaign. Its deployment was restricted to the Baltic and Black Seas.

Although Operation *Barbarossa* was primarily a land war and although this was where the German Armed Forces had felt at home since time immemorial, the war also rapidly exposed the weak links in the *Wehrmacht*'s professionalism. It was in this endurance test that it became apparent how improvised the German forces truly were. They had been shrunk to merely 115,000 men between 1919 and 1933, after which a rearmament programme had begun in which those cadres were divided again and again so as to have their numbers supplemented with hundreds of thousands of conscripts, volunteers, and reactivated veterans of the First World War, all furnished with first German and then increasingly captured military equipment, which, however, proved less and less equal to demand, in both quantity and quality. The result was ultimately a complex conglomerate of units and divisions that differed greatly in professionalism, equipment, and attitudes.

The backbone of the German Eastern Army consisted of the Infantry Divisions, thoroughly capable units of over 17,000 men whose provision with vehicles, anti-tank guns, and heavy weapons was, however, all too limited. Since the Infantry Divisions soon lost their modest pool of vehicles, they marched and fought as in the Napoleonic era—on foot or by horse and cart, with rifles and artillery. The German Eastern Army began Operation *Barbarossa* with 750,000 horses; during the course of the war, the demand for this archaic form of transport grew steadily, along with the concomitant need for carts.

The Eastern Army's 3,350 panzers and 600,000 motor vehicles (in June 1941) had instead been concentrated largely in the Motorized Divisions. These few elite groups were to tear open the enemy's front line and so make a blitzkrieg possible. The German armies at the time were rightly compared to a lance—a piercing, hard, short point on a long wooden shaft. With a relatively small arsenal of modern weapons—that is, armoured vehicles of all sorts, motorized artillery, rocket launchers, modern radio and permanent air support—the *Wehrmacht* was able to produce the local superiority that swung battles—rapid raids independent of the infantry's marching speed. But this potential was soon exhausted, actually as soon as autumn 1941.

Also insufficient right from the first were the units intended to control the enormous occupied zone. The soldiers deployed here were those who were no use at the front: the older year groups or those with some slight physical impairment. Their training was poor. 'The great mass of the battalion has never fired live rounds,' complained the leader of one of these divisions in spring 1942. And these Security Divisions, which were weaker than their regular Infantry equivalents in both men and material, were supposed to patrol a gigantic occupied zone the majority of which was completely undeveloped. A Security Division of around 10,000 men could be responsible for an area of around 40,000 square kilometres, an area half the size of Scotland. It is easy to see that their mission was a futile one.

The best way to visualize the organization and proportions of the Eastern Army is perhaps a breakdown of the forces in June 1943. At that point, there were 217 German divisions deployed on the Eastern Front, of which 154 were infantry, 37 motorized, and only 26 allocated for maintaining the military occupation. Truly modern battle groups able to call on the whole repertoire of modern armaments remained the exception. This also draws attention to something else that would be important later: most German soldiers experienced the war at the front and not in the hinterland.

The Eastern Army had to absorb terrible losses as early as summer 1941. For an army that was lacking strength in depth and particularly reserves of personnel, that was catastrophic. Without the help of Germany's allies, even the summer offensive of 1942 would not have been possible. Nonetheless, from 1943 the Eastern Army was supposed to experience a kind of 'second spring' after the beginning of the 'armaments miracle' presided over by Albert Speer. It was only then that the heavier and technologically modern panzers were put into action—the Tiger, the Panther, and the various tank hunters. With the introduction of assault rifles and the anti-tank *panzerfaust* in 1944–5, the infantry also began to hit harder. But by then it was too late for this modernization drive to alter the course of the war.

From winter 1941–2 onwards, the Eastern Army was living from hand to mouth both militarily and logistically. Its situation was defined by the continuous improvisation with which it managed to postpone the great military catastrophe until summer 1944. What rescued the divisions fighting in the East time and again were their cohesion and their professional ability, along with good troop leadership. That compensated for a lot—for their horrendous losses, their increasing immobility, the ever more bizarre instructions from the *Führer* headquarters, and, finally, the growing superiority of their opponent. As early as 1941, a German regimental commander found the battles so fierce that 'the German soldiers who survived were hardened into as powerful a troop such as we have rarely had'. They were unusually cohesive, and desertions remained very rare on the Eastern Front until the winter of 1944–5. The reasons for that were doubtless a tough diet of authority and obedience, along with an enemy whom most of the *Landsers*, the ordinary troops, rightly feared. Even more effective were the attitudes that ensured their continued commitment to such ideals as comradeship, courage, and the fatherland, and so also to the world of military organization. On top of that, the lie disseminated by German propagandists, that the attack on the Soviet Union had been a pre-emptive strike, was long believed, particularly under the influence of a Nazi ideology whose mechanisms of social engineering had succeeded in leaving their imprint especially on the younger soldiers.

In general, the perspectives of the *Wehrmacht* soldiers were far more diverse than one would initially imagine, often simply because it consisted of differing generations. Of greater consequence was that these men's attitudes necessarily changed under the pressure of a war whose reality corresponded ever less closely to the grandiloquent promises of German propaganda. In the end all this was outweighed by the knowledge or suspicion of their own guilt, whether individually or nationally, and also by the conviction that their homes had to be defended against the 'Bolsheviks', simply because the front now ran right through their own homeland. That, too, explains why the German Eastern Army never disintegrated. But soldiers do not usually have the opportunity to determine their own actions, and those actions cannot be explained just by the soldiers' thinking. The external factors were far more powerful: the army, the dictatorship, and a war by which the soldiers were held captive—no less so than their Soviet enemies.

Allies

It is often overlooked that the German invaders did not fight alone in the Soviet Union; by their side stood many allies from throughout Europe. In 1943, every third man in uniform on the German side was not a German. 'It can hardly have been more colourful in the medieval armies,' as one German medic said of his 'Cavalry Squadron East', which recruited from Red Army prisoners of war. There were various reasons why the Eastern Army became an international force; it was a consequence of both state agreements and individual decisions, and so there were allied troops, European volunteers, and local collaborators.

This had not been envisaged. Particularly in a war such as this one, Hitler wanted to retain the maximum possible freedom of decision, which entailed not having to take account of allies whom experience had shown to be often weak or difficult. Only two states were supposed really to participate in the great Eastern conquest: Finland and Romania. Although both pursued territorial interests within the Soviet Union, they did not infringe on the German sphere because they were engaged only at the furthest peripheries of the Eastern Front, in regions that would have anyway presented problems for the *Wehrmacht*. The Romanian and especially the Finnish armies thus maintained a relatively high level of autonomy. The other partners Hitler desired, Turkey and

Bulgaria, were sufficiently perspicacious to keep themselves out of this undertaking, Turkey entirely, Bulgaria on the whole.

There was little room for any other allies in Hitler's plans for his future *Lebensraum*. This made things far from simple, not least because the German invasion of the USSR was very popular in some parts of Europe; it tapped into a significant anti-Bolshevik impulse, a passion for war, and a naked greed for the spoils of conquest. 'Your decision to take Russia by the throat has met with enthusiastic approval in Italy,' Mussolini telegraphed to Hitler in summer 1941. Italy, Hungary, Slovakia, and Croatia, all official German allies, did not miss the opportunity to be among the first divisions entering the Soviet theatre of war. Mainly third rate in their training and equipment, these troops were initially left in the lee of larger military events.

Only in 1942, when the German leadership realized how dependent it was on outside help, were whole armies of Romanians, Italians, and Hungarians included in the second German offensive. They were to pay a high price for being so hopelessly out of their depth, and their German partners seldom showed any gratitude for their contribution. After the debacle of Stalingrad, it was bitterly recorded on the Italian side that their own soldiers had starved while the Germans provided them with 'not the slightest assistance'. 'If an Italian soldier approached a German kitchen and asked for a little food or water, he was greeted with pistol shots.' In total, 800,000 Hungarians, 500,000 Finns, 500,000 Romanians, 250,000 Italians, 145,000 Croats, and 45,000 Slovakians fought in the Soviet Union. Most of them were there because they had been ordered to go.

The rest of Europe, by contrast, was represented by volunteers. Their contingents were far smaller and more heterogeneous, but, as a rule, also more motivated. For them, taking up arms on behalf of Germany—out of political conviction, a lust for adventure, or a need for belonging and social advancement—was a personal choice. The Germans first reacted reluctantly, despite the lip service they paid to shared ideology. But opinions soon changed as German losses mounted, and they began to overlook the fact that the racial criteria of Nazism were supposed to apply equally to foreign volunteers. The German recruiters initially distinguished between 'non-Germanic' volunteers, such as Spaniards, Croats, or Frenchmen, who mainly became part of the *Wehrmacht*, and 'Germanic' volunteers, Danes, Norwegians, or Dutchmen, who were usually assigned to the Waffen SS so as to form the core of a future 'Pan-Germanic Army'. This was also the destination for the huge supply of ethnic Germans living outside Germany, most of them in south-east Europe. The majority, however, ended up in the army, not as volunteers, but because of international bilateral agreements. Although the Germans significantly intensified the propaganda aimed at recruitment, not least because of the great symbolic and political value of a united Europe fighting against Russia, the results fell far short of what they hoped. The numbers of foreign volunteers deployed on the Eastern Front between 1941 and 1945 are estimated as the following: 47,000 Spaniards, 40,000 Dutchmen, 38,000 Belgians, 20,000 Poles, 10,000 Frenchmen, 6,000 Norwegians, and 4,000 Danes, as well as smaller groups of Finns, Swedes, Portuguese, and Swiss.

The final group, of a quite different military and political significance, was made up of the collaborators. The figures alone make that clear. It is estimated that 800,000 Russians, 280,000 people from the Caucasus, 250,000 Ukrainians, 100,000 Latvians, 60,000 Estonians, 47,000 Byelorussians, and 20,000 Lithuanians bore arms on the German side. This happened, again, for a range of varied reasons. For the soldiers from the Baltic, the Caucasus, and the Ukraine, nationalist and anti-Bolshevik motives played an important role; while the appearance of Russians, mainly as 'Hiwis' (*Hilfswillige*, voluntary assistants), was often the result of coercion or straightforward need, and only secondarily as a consequence of personal conviction or political commitment.

Just as heterogeneous as the origins and mentalities of these military collaborators were their willingness and ability to fight. Looking back on them, one of their German commanders wrote that a fifth 'were good, a fifth bad and the other three-fifths inconsistent'. This became even more obvious because they were grouped together by nationality, first the Baltic soldiers, then the people of the Caucasus, the Ukrainians, and, by the end of the war, the Russians, too, in the so-called Russian Liberation Army. Nevertheless, odd remnants of an imagined European crusade against Bolshevism were able to outlive the downfall of Nazi Germany. There were exiles and right-wing extremists who continued eagerly to propagate these fantasies after 1945, as well as a number of scattered anti-Bolshevik guerrilla groups that maintained their activities in the Baltic countries and the Ukraine until well into the 1950s.

The real problem with all of this was that any form of military or political power-sharing was in diametrical opposition to the course plotted by the Nazi leadership. Their plans would have alienated even the most enthusiastic collaborators, because Hitler remained fundamentally indifferent to the 'hearts and minds' of his helpers from Eastern Europe, though it was precisely those Eastern Europeans who could have been the most important. The *Führer*, despite all propaganda material to the contrary, was stubbornly unwilling, right to the last, to make use of the opportunity they presented and come up with a viable political concept to underpin the oft-trumpeted 'New European Order'. Although elements of the *Wehrmacht*, the ministerial bureaucracy, and even the SS High Command increasingly came to rely on them, the Eastern European collaborators were kept on a short leash, entirely dependent on German instructions.

Nevertheless, the fight against the Soviet Union was not Hitler's war alone. Ultimately, it was a German war that was also, to some extent, a European one, in which many expectations and intentions were bundled together, some of them entirely incompatible with one other.

The Soviet Union's land and people

It seemed almost endless, the country that the *Wehrmacht* invaded in summer 1941, and that was another reason for the German defeat: 21.8 million square kilometres, a sixth of the earth, as Soviet propaganda used proudly to announce. Just as sobering for the *Wehrmacht* as the size of the Soviet Union was its climate. Its greater part was classified as within the temperate zone (alongside smaller arctic, subarctic, and subtropical areas), which meant that the summers, at least, were sometimes bearable for the combatants, but then summer could also bring sweltering heat, choking dust, and drought, or otherwise cataclysmic downpours, unending mud, and myriads of mosquitoes. The winter, however, was uniformly horrific. It bit into all the soldiers, regardless of whether they were deployed in Lapland or the Crimea, and was especially difficult to endure because large parts of the Soviet Union were still almost wild and far more sparsely inhabited than the German

Reich. In Germany, there were 131 people per square kilometre, in the Ukraine there were 69, in Belorussia 44, and in Russia itself just 7.

In total, however, the Soviet population was enormous. In 1939, there were 167 million people; in 1941, this had grown to 194 million, largely as a result of annexations. That in itself presented the *Wehrmacht* with a grave problem: how to win a war against an enemy whose resources of manpower were practically inexhaustible. The nature of Soviet society did, on the other hand, also offer the German strategists one great advantage and possible solution to the problem—it was not ethnically homogeneous, but was instead divided between around 60 peoples and 100 smaller groups. In the First World War, the German side had tried, not without success, to turn the Russian Empire's own peoples against it by adopting policies that supported national independence movements. This was a strategy the German High Command could have employed once again. Could have, that is, since Hitler and his followers had quite other plans for these people. Nonetheless, particularly in the farther-flung corners of the Soviet empire, there existed a latent readiness to cooperate with the Germans that was not the result solely of nationalism. Another reason was what the people had experienced of their Bolshevik rulers. The Bolsheviks had had twenty years to make a reality of the new kind of society they had promised, though the conditions could hardly have been more difficult. The proletarian revolution had occurred in the country that Marxist orthodoxy would perhaps have judged least ready for it—in a vast, technologically underdeveloped empire that was extremely backward both socially and politically as well as deeply marked by the Tsar, the aristocracy, the Church, and an ancient peasant culture whose daily round was almost untouched by the goings-on in Moscow or St Petersburg. There were additional obstacles, first among them the inheritance of defeat in the First World War and of the Civil War in Russia itself, one long tragedy of violence, hunger, and deprivation that, between 1914 and 1921, had cost the lives of some 11.5 million people. Another was the ethnic fragmentation of a Soviet Union that placed too little worth on the internationalism that formed part of its doctrine; and, lastly, there was the long, painful coming-of-age of the Bolsheviks themselves after Lenin's early death (17 January 1924), a process at the end of which stood what Lenin had warned against from his deathbed: the dictatorship of Stalin.

It was Stalin who was truly to revolutionize the country. Under his rule, the peasantry, the largest social group, shrank significantly, from 72 per cent (1926) to 51 per cent (1941). Even more momentous was that almost all peasants simultaneously lost their independence. During the programme of enforced collectivization, they became 'agricultural workers' on almost 250,000 *kolkhozy* (collective farms) or *sovkhozy* (state farms). The tremendous haste with which agricultural nationalization was driven along had a fundamentally damaging effect on living and working conditions. In the former breadbasket of Europe, many basic foodstuffs were rationed until 1935. The privation was worst in the countryside, where between five and seven million people starved to death in the early 1930s. This catastrophe was accompanied by the deportation and execution of those whom the Soviet terror apparatus believed to be standing in the way of Stalin's ambitious advance towards modernity.

The focus of his politics was the industrial sector, not the agricultural. The latter's collectivization was seen as merely a first step. The old village culture was to disappear; the people were to move to the towns and there be transformed into industrial workers, while the remaining 'agricultural factories' finally managed to guarantee sufficient food supplies and even use a new surplus to finance the growth of heavy industry. That was the grand project. Stalin wanted to make up in one decade for an economic lag that he himself estimated at 'fifty to a hundred years'. How to do so was detailed in the Five Year Plans, first announced in 1929. As if it were possible simply to command that the economy grow, Soviet society was mobilized, made responsible for reaching the targets dictated to it, and thrown into ever more productivity drives, which did indeed give some parts of the country a modern appearance. New industrial concerns and factory towns appeared, along with blast furnaces, canals, tractors, and vast water reservoirs. One statistic after another celebrated the 'construction of socialism', and, even if that was still limited to a single country, victory over capitalism was declared nonetheless. Much of that was unfounded propaganda, but not all, as Soviet gross domestic product increased by 50 per cent between 1928 and 1940, and a basis was laid for the growth of heavy industry. Not only did the economy change; there emerged a new breed of proletariatians, young and mobile, with a high ratio of women and far more open to the slogans of socialism than their peasant parents had been. Between 1926 and 1937, the proportion of industrial workers in Soviet society was multiplied tenfold, from 3 per cent to 31 per cent. It was a huge effort, almost *ex nihilo*, and it allowed the Soviet Union gradually to become an industrial and then a military power, as well as turning it into a country that corresponded at least in outline to the Bolshevik conception of what society ought to be. It was enough to make many believe in the utopian vision of a new, equitable world to come. Despite all the bungling and the profligacy, the economic trend was directed very distinctly upwards.

But the price was high. This huge effort to which almost everything was sacrificed—capital, workers, resources—came at the cost of sustainability, quality, and individual consumer goods, as well as doing unprecedented structural damage to the Soviet economy. Even more serious was the abyss of violence in which the socio-economic revolution was forced through. There is no question that the Bolshevik regime had been accompanied by violence from the first and that its use was not a new phenomenon. During the Civil War, the Red Terror had already claimed 280,000 victims. Its conception of the enemy had even then been a broad church: spies, counter-revolutionaries, saboteurs, the bourgeoisie, 'enemies of the people', priests, kulaks, and all members of all non-Bolshevik parties or national autonomy movements.

But it was under Stalin that the politics of repression, murder, and 'liquidation' reached their height. Between five and seven million people lost their lives during the enforced collectivization of agriculture at the start of the 1930s, particularly in the Ukraine, along the Don and Kuban rivers, an area from around which a further 1.8 million people were deported. This was followed after 1935 by the deportation of individual ethnic groups and the continuing persecution of the kulaks, relatively affluent farmers, 273,000 of whom were killed. Then came the Great Terror of the years 1937–8, which was directed primarily at administrative and military officials. Some 1.5 million people were arrested and at least 680,000 executed. Finally, 480,000 people from the Sovietized western provinces were deported or murdered between 1939 and 1941. These were undoubtedly extreme examples of Stalin's governance, but a permanent war against his own society was an essential characteristic of the regime. He demanded, this was the crux, that society be the way he imagined it, a way that in reality it never was. The consequence was an uninterrupted series of inspections, show trials, arrests, deportations, and 'purges' of his own administration, accompanied by the construction of a gigantic network of prison camps, the notorious Gulag Archipelago. The Gulag became a dark parallel society living in the shadow of the Bolshevik upswing that Stalin announced in 1935 had made life 'better' and 'happier'. For the eighteen million people who passed through the Gulag under his dictatorship, it was certainly neither; as early as 1941, two million had succumbed to the inhuman conditions. Taking these into account, there is a large body of evidence to suggest that, between 1927 and 1941, Stalin's politics claimed the lives of some ten million people.

At the outbreak of war, Stalinist Russia thus had far more on its conscience than Nazi Germany. The latter would, however, do much throughout the rest of its short existence to make up the deficit. To understand this as a reaction to Soviet atrocities would be fundamentally misguided. The criminal character of both regimes was inherent in their ideologies, their mentalities, and also in their organizations; they were two separate and self-contained systems with their own sets of historical and political preconditions. In Poland alone, the German occupiers had shot more than 60,000 people by the end of 1939. That these two totalitarian regimes would then reciprocally influence and radicalize each other in their fight to the death was almost an inevitability. However, their actions were still generally determined by what they had brought with them into the war: ideologies that treated such principles as tolerance, individuality, and the rule of law with nothing but contempt.

The defenders

The Soviet Armed Forces also found themselves in a period of upheaval. By the early 1940s, little remained of their origins in the dramatic years of the Bolshevik Revolution and the Civil War: the political symbolism, perhaps, and the system of having commissars shadow the officers, as well as a few commanders whose careers had begun in 1917. But it was precisely in the officer corps that it was evident how much the Red Army had changed. The officers had been among the first victims of the purges that took place between 1937 and 1940. Of the 5 Marshals of the Soviet Union, 3 'disappeared', along with 29 of the thirty army commanders and commissars, and 110 of the 195 division commanders. In total, of the 899 highest-ranking officers, 643 were persecuted and 583 killed. In all, about 100,000 ordinary soldiers were subject to some form of repression. This was no coincidence. Although the Workers' and Peasants' Red Army, as it was officially called, had been at the disposal of a dictatorship since its inception, it had still been allowed a certain professional autonomy. Now, however, the guiding mentality made an abrupt about-turn. Now it was important above all to toe the political line and that meant total orientation on the *vozhd*, Stalin.

That was not the only change. What is also striking about the period before the war is the Soviet Armed Forces' exponential growth. From 529,000 men (1924) to more than 1.3 million (1935–6), it had reached a total of 5.3 million men by 1941, around half of whom were stationed on the western border. Another twelve million men were available as reserves. This explosive expansion was accompanied by an acceleration of material provision in which, it has to be said, sheer volume of equipment was prized above its efficacy. Nonetheless, at the outbreak of war, the Red Army had an enormous arsenal at its disposal: 23,000 tanks, more than 115,900 heavy guns and mortars, and 13,300 usable aeroplanes. There is no doubt that it had become one of the most powerful armies in the world, even if the Soviet leadership continued to make the mistake of confusing quantity with quality. But at that point—and this was the salient fact—they did not really expect to be fighting a major war, not least because the record of the few Soviet deployments before summer 1941 was decidedly patchy. In the small Manchurian border disputes, they had gained the upper hand against the Japanese (1938–9) and just about managed to succeed in conquering the half of Poland allocated them, but the war against Finland had very nearly ended in fiasco. This, too, seemed to indicate that the Red Army could not be considered battle ready before summer 1942 at the earliest.

The German invasion struck them with a terrible shock. The dominant sentiment of the Soviet defenders in the first months of the war can have been nothing but fear: fear of the apparently invincible supremacy of the German invaders; fear of control by the political cadres, who initially thought it would be possible to manage an army like a party organization; fear of the officers, who callously threw away the lives of their troops; fear of the indolence in the supply lines that meant what was really needed did not reach the front; and, not least, fear of death, which soon became terribly familiar to the Soviet troops. More than 3.5 million of them did not survive the first year of the war. One officer of the German High Command wrote in his diary that 'the

Russians sacrifice their people and they sacrifice themselves in a way that Western Europeans can hardly imagine'.

And yet, the Red Army was collectively able to bring the *Wehrmacht* to a halt. There were many reasons for that: the Soviet Union's almost inexhaustible reserves, the steadily improving quality of their armaments from autumn 1941, the knowledge that they were fighting a just cause, and, finally, the lessons learned in the hard school of war in which the soldiers of the Red Army had no choice but to enrol. Although their losses were horrendous, although the Red Army lost the majority of its heavy weaponry in the first months of the war, a new army emerged that was vastly superior, in both quantity and quality, to that of 1941. A proud Soviet political officer wrote of the army's operations in 1943 that 'even the Germans in 1941 were never as good as this'. Two years earlier, he had ended up among the partisans after the destruction of his unit and had lived to see regular Soviet divisions fight their way through to him and his comrades.

At that moment, in autumn 1943, the Soviet Armed Forces consisted of 13.2 million people in total, 5.5 million of them fighting on what for the Soviet Union was the Western Front. By the end of the war, the Soviet Union had mobilized 30.6 million soldiers, 820,000 of them women. Their equipment, too, changed beyond recognition. The Red Army became more mobile, largely because of the tens of thousands of vehicles that arrived from the USA and Great Britain, but, most important of all, it learned to hit harder. The most feared Soviet weapons of the Second World War were the T-34 tank, the heavy guns, the PPSh-41 submachine gun with its distinctive drum magazine, the Katyusha rocket launcher, the mortars, and an artillery that grew into a rolling thunder of regiments, divisions, and even whole artillery armies the like of which the world had never seen. Stalin thought of them as embodying the god of war. Finally, there was the air force; in 1941, its machines were swept from the sky by their German enemies or destroyed while still on the ground. At the beginning of 1943, the tide turned, and aerial dominance became the privilege of the Soviets. That was not simply because of their new machines, which were stronger and more modern. 'Against ten of us there were often three hundred Russians,' remembered one German fighter pilot. 'You were just as likely to have a mid-air collision as to be shot down.'

The fatal blow, however, was struck on the ground. By that point, the Red Army's soldiers were professional, confident, and highly motivated. 'I can be proud', wrote a lieutenant in October 1942, 'that the battlefield is covered in Krauts I've personally killed and counted off...'. What came to matter in the army was no longer class background and political loyalty, but ability and action. The Party and the state also learned to make use of the deeply rooted patriotism that had lain dormant in Soviet society. They created Guards Regiments, uniforms reminiscent of the old Russia, and an elaborate system of honours. There was little talk of internationalism in this hour of need. Confronted with the nature of the German occupation, most of the soldiers must have been entirely convinced of the reason for their deployment—most, but not all, because Soviet society always remained politically and ethnically far more heterogeneous than its leadership would have cared to admit. A sophisticated surveillance apparatus, the system of assigning certain battalions for punishment or using them to prevent others retreating, as well as summary executions, all remained part of the military everyday, along with a High Command that used the people entrusted to it with a shocking wastefulness. Even at the beginning of 1945, one in sixteen Red Army soldiers captured by the *Wehrmacht* was a deserter. This ambivalence—boundless devotion and enthusiasm, but also indoctrination, control, terror, and an unprecedented profligacy with human life—all these characterized the situation of the Soviet military. The sole aim was to win the war—regardless of the price that would be paid, above all, by its soldiers.

4

War 1941–1942

The war from above: overview

There are few subjects as historiographically difficult and challenging as the description of war. That applies particularly to its epicentre, to the actual fighting. There are a great many people involved, as well as enormous, complex organizations; there is a permanent alternation between high drama and phases of crushing tedium; there are the intensely emotive subjects of death, defeat, and blame; and there are necessarily two contrary perspectives that often seem incommensurable. In the case of a war as large and also as extreme as the German–Soviet one, merely sketching an overview of the military operations presents a challenge. In 1942, these took place on a front that stretched 3,000 kilometres through the Soviet Union. Of the innumerable engagements that were played out, many have by now been entirely forgotten, even though tens or even hundreds of thousands of soldiers were involved.

In the midst of this apparent chaos, however, it is possible to make out certain patterns. One is determined by the seasons. The great German offensives always took place in summer, those of the Red Army initially only in winter. And there is something else that catches the historian's eye: German offensive capabilities shrank from year to year. Whereas the *Wehrmacht* attacked along the whole length of the front in 1941, in 1942 it did so with only one Army Group; in 1943, with two smaller armies, and, finally, in summer 1944, none of the German forces in the East was able to advance from its position. Now that its opponent had seized the initiative during the Germans' favoured season, it could no longer be recovered. Casting an eye over the Soviet operations, on the other hand, rapidly makes clear the extent to which the war was a learning process for the Red Army, on all levels of military thinking—tactically, strategically, and operationally. It continued to make dreadful errors right until the end, and those errors contributed as much as anything to the horrendous losses that it suffered.

A second organizing idea in this tremendous military struggle is that of territory. War is always partly a geographical phenomenon. Territory, in a sense, provides the parameters; it gives an unmistakable indication of the two opponents' successes or failures. This is particularly true of a war such as that in the Soviet Union. Of course, it is often overlooked that this conflict was not only a war of manœuvre. Long stretches of the front fought a war of attrition that outwardly at least was reminiscent of the First World War. But, even then, the military events were not confined to the comparatively narrow band of two parallel front lines. In a contest characterized by limitless violence, it was inevitable that the hinterland, too, would become a war zone. Nevertheless, the war was decided by what happened at the front, along the main lines of battle. Everything else was dependent on that. That is why an operational history remains indispensable to understanding the course of the war. The thin line of the front formed the axis around which all else turned.

1941: the German invasion

Bright and early on 22 June 1941, a sunny Sunday morning, the Wehrmacht crossed the border. There had not been a declaration of war; it was a surprise attack. That was one of the key reasons why it seemed that the German troops would soon add the Soviet Union to their list of conquests. Stalin had repeatedly been warned about the build-up to Operation *Barbarossa* but had consistently refused to put the Red Army into defensive readiness. Instead, his High Command had concentrated the majority of its forces on the border, because Soviet doctrine stipulated that, in the event of an attack, the army was immediately to carry the war onto enemy soil. Nonetheless, or in fact precisely for that reason, the four German panzer groups quickly succeeded in breaking through the Soviet positions, forming the first 'cauldrons', encirclements of enemy armies, and managed to advance 400 kilometres into Soviet territory within a single week. For the German infantry armies following along behind in that hot, dusty summer, that meant: marching, more marching and then 'clearing' one cauldron after another. Soviet prisoners were soon being counted in the hundreds of thousands.

The German leadership was triumphant. Before the outbreak of war, it had had a nagging fear that the enemy units would—as in 1812—fall back into their country's interior and refuse to give battle. That had obviously not come to pass. On the contrary, the toughness of Soviet resistance seemed to confirm the assumptions

ILLUSTRATION 3. German soldiers examine a captured Soviet KV II tank, July 1941

on which the German strategy was built. On 28 June, German troops conquered Minsk, the capital of Belorussia; on 15 July, they were already at the gates of Smolensk. In three weeks, the distance between Army Group Centre and Moscow had thus shrunk from over 1,000 to around 350 kilometres. 'In our mind's eye, we can already see the towers of the Kremlin,' exulted the members of one German infantry regiment. Even the head of the German General Staff, Franz Halder, believed at the start of July that 'the campaign against Russia will be won within a fortnight'. He was not the only one of this opinion. In Great Britain and the USA, the Soviet military had already been written off. One British general wrote, 'I fear they will be herded together like cattle.'

But this belief ran counter to all military experience. According to the old rule of thumb, it is only with a three-to-one advantage that victory is assured. Since in this case the defenders in fact retained numerical superiority and continued on the whole (though not always) to fight hard and bitterly, the German troops, pushing ever farther into the unending emptiness of the steppe, began to win their victories on the point of exhaustion. This could be seen in their losses, which were particularly dire in the battles to break through Soviet lines as a prelude to encirclement, and it could be seen in what was happening to their equipment. Before long, more German vehicles were being lost to dust, mud, and the catastrophic roads than to the enemy. In August 1941, an officer in a German Infantry Division noted that the East was now beginning 'to show its true face'. The German armies were not prepared for what they now encountered. Reserves of everything were short, and the supplies of fuel, rations, ammunition, and spare parts, to say nothing of vehicles proper, began to run out after only the first weeks. A decisive battle no longer seemed probable, and the

Germans began to lose their taste for the word *Blitzkrieg*, the lightning war. When Chief of Staff Halder was forced to confess, on 11 August, that 'we have underestimated the Russian colossus', the consternation among the leadership was already palpable. Even then, they were no longer really sure what to do next.

What followed were heated discussions in the *Führer* HQ about the future focal points of the German offensive. This question, like so much else, had initially been left unresolved. While Hitler wanted above all to occupy the Soviet centres of industry and raw material, and thus favoured the two wings of the three more-or-less equally strong Army Groups—that is, 'North' and 'South'—it was clear to his military advisers that that could not happen before a decisive victory had been won in the field. Only an attack on Moscow, on the centre of the enormous Soviet empire, seemed likely to provide it. There is no doubt that the loss of the capital would have been a powerful blow to the Soviet enemy. However, it does also seem questionable whether a war of this scale and kind could have been ended with a single 'decisive' manœuvre. It was almost as though the German military, in near desperation, were clutching at this one tangible goal merely so as to make sense of an increasingly unmanageable campaign. And not only that. For the exhausted and disillusioned soldiers who were already 'thoroughly sick of Russia'—as one soldier wrote as early as August—Moscow presented a large and apparently convincing target. Its name was a promise of victory, and even perhaps of a speedy end to the conflict.

Hitler's ability to assert himself over his advisers in the making of these plans demonstrates the extent to which he by now also dominated operational strategy. When he, in August, switched the focal point of the German offensive from Moscow to the south-east, it resulted in another great success for the *Wehrmacht*—at least on the face of things. In a cauldron outside Kiev, a further 665,000 Red Army troops had laid down their arms by the end of September. It was one of the Red Army's largest and most comprehensive defeats. But neither that nor the conquest of the Ukrainian capital provided a military turning point. In September, the increasingly perplexed *Führer* therefore decided to attack Moscow after all, even though the conditions had altered and it was now far later in the year.

It was only on 2 October 1941 that the Eastern Army was in a position to launch its supposedly final onslaught. Seventy-eight divisions, nearly two million men, had been gathered in the centre for Operation *Typhoon*. Chief of Staff Halder wrote that it was finally time to 'break the back' of the Red Army. And, indeed, by 20 October the Soviet side had lost 673,000 soldiers and almost 1,300 tanks in the twin battles of Vyazma and Bryansk. By December, individual German units had managed to fight their way to within 30 kilometres of the Soviet capital. But now it was also becoming unmistakable how severely the German Eastern Army had been depleted by the offensive. The change of weather in autumn had already made things difficult: rain and then snow transformed the Russian roads into a grey, bottomless morass into which whole armies sank. By mid-October, the entire Army Group Centre was stuck fast 'in mud and sludge', as their Commander in Chief, Field Marshal Fedor von Bock, noted with chagrin.

In November came winter, bringing catastrophe in its wake. Since the High Command had organized winter provisions for only a small occupying army, most of the German soldiers continued to fight in their tattered summer uniforms. One of them

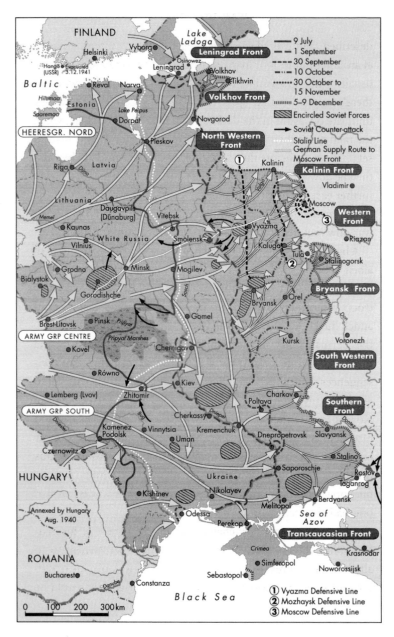

MAP 2. The Eastern Front in 1941

described their everyday existence as follows: 'The men wake up at around three or four in the morning and get ready to move out, usually without washing, because the water is too far away and there's no time and no light. The marching then goes on all day until late on, again in the dark, often at nine or ten o'clock, when the men reach their quarters and have to care for the horses and set up the stalls before they have their mess at the field kitchen and then lie down to sleep.' Nevertheless, the soldiers were driven ever further east by their commanders—in the putative hope that the Soviet enemy had already been essentially beaten and that all that was now required was a last, decisive 'battle of annihilation'.

A battle of this type did indeed begin on the 5–6 December 1941, albeit moving in the other direction. German intelligence had completely failed to notice that the Red Army had brought up new troop reserves after realizing, in November, that Japan would attack the USA rather than the USSR. The Soviet offensive struck the German units, already thinned out and dead tired, in the moment of greatest weakness, that of a stalled offensive. The consequences were as one would expect. In temperatures that fell to −52 °C, Army Group Centre was propelled a distance of between 150 and 300 kilometres to the west. Nothing was as strongly reminiscent of Napoleon's Russian campaign, the military disaster par excellence, as the image of German columns struggling westwards through snow and ice. 'For days on end, the wind whipped up the fine, powdery snow and drove it into our eyes and faces, so that one had the feeling of having stumbled into a rain of needles,' wrote a German military chaplain about the retreat of his division. 'Since the storms came mainly from the east, the enemy usually had them at his back. It was easy for him to move his troops forward under the cover of snow clouds so that they would be noticed only at the last moment.' By the end, in his unit 'approximately 70 per cent of the troops had frostbite, partly third degree'. Their commanders' prognosis was equally bleak: 'Fighting capability of the troops is zero, as completely exhausted.'

This was no 'straightening of the front', as was claimed by the Reich's propagandists. The whole German Eastern Front was in danger of collapse. That it did not come to that was not only because of the cohesion, skill, and toughness of troops who knew that they were fighting for their lives. It was also due to the grave errors still being made by the Stavka, the Soviet High Command. It did not manage to gather its forces and concentrate them on a small number of crucial targets. From February onwards, the Soviet attacks were increasingly ragged and ever more Red Army troops died pointlessly in front of the German lines. It was not rare to find that battles were reduced to a 'fight for an oven', a scrap over the few villages that remained intact in the desert of snow. When the fronts then sank into the bottomless mud of spring 1942, both sides were equally glad of the break. It lasted long enough for the German front, which now ran straight across Russia and the Ukraine, from the area around Leningrad to the Black Sea, to be at least partly consolidated. That, however, was the only gain made. Hitler's strategy, the plan of a worldwide blitzkrieg, had definitively failed, so definitively that the German Reich had almost gone under—as early as that, in winter 1941–2. The prospects for the future were not much brighter. Instead of winning itself strategic freedom of action, the German High Command now found itself having to manage a war on two fronts at a time when it was already evident how overextended its forces were. 'We have been punished for overestimating our strength and for our hubris,' read the assessment of an officer in the German

General Staff in December 1941. 'If only we can distil some lessons from the events of the last months.'

1942: the second German offensive

Learning lessons was something Hitler would not do. He would not be wrested from his principle of escalating the odds in the face of risk. After the Eastern Army had, by 1942, suffered losses of over a million killed, wounded, and missing, an attack along the length of the front was no longer possible. Instead, there would be an attack along one section in the south. All reserves and all supplies were scratched together; where they were insufficient, the Germans' allies had to make up the shortfall. Time was short because, since 11 December 1941, the German Reich had also found itself at war with the USA. If there was to be any chance at all for the Reich, Hitler thought it would lie in the Caucasus. Before American armament production could start to run at full capacity, the German Reich would annex the military potential of the Soviet Union. In order to do so, the summer offensive was planned in two phases: it would first advance onto the Volga at Stalingrad, then—after building up an east-facing front—wheel around towards the Caucasus so as to take possession of the Soviet oil-fields. Without them, the Soviet Union—so hoped the Germans— would collapse.

The German offensive began on 28 June 1942. After a number of preliminary battles—around Kharkov, Izium, and on the Crimean peninsula, which the Germans had occupied by 1 July— four German armies, supported by Hungarian, Romanian, and Italian divisions, initiated Operation *Blue*. Again, the attackers made rapid territorial gains. But now, and increasingly often, their

ILLUSTRATION 4. Marching East: German infantry cross the River Don, 1 August 1942

offensives ran on and on into an enormous void, because Stalin, after long hesitation, had eventually given his commanders permission for a tactical withdrawal. Given the paltry numbers of Soviet prisoners taken, Field Marshal von Bock remarked that there was danger of having 'struck at thin air'. Hitler was not receptive to such doubts and permitted less and less outside involvement in his operational leadership. Believing that the enemy had now been beaten at last, he split the German offensive and directed the armies simultaneously, rather than one after the other, towards Stalingrad and the Caucasus. At first, this fateful decision could hardly slow the pace of the German advance. Churning up thick clouds of dust, the troops marched ever further east across the shadowless steppe, crossing the border into Asia at the end of July and reaching the burning, destroyed refineries of Maykop at the start of August. On the 22nd of that month, German alpine troops raised the Reich's war flag above the Elbrus, the highest mountain in the Caucasus. Days later, the Sixth Army's first reconnaissance units were standing on the banks of the Volga, north of Stalingrad. Never before had the Germans ruled over such an enormous territory.

And then everything stopped. Now, if not before, the German leadership had indubitably expended or worn out the last of its resources; one German major wrote that his troops had already been 'stripped of all but their shirts'. The tormenting question of the previous weeks, of how long the Soviet Union would hold up against this renewed onslaught, began to be answered slowly and almost imperceptibly. At first the Germans noticed only that the battles in the ancient forests of the Caucasus moraine and in the stone deserts of Stalingrad were beginning to bite. The battle on the Volga, in particular, developed into a duel between the dictators, a matter of prestige that sucked in more and more troops. On 28 July, Stalin gave his famous order: 'Not one step back!' In a public speech on 8 November, Hitler replied that the battle for Stalingrad had basically already been decided. But that victory could not be talked into existence. The German intelligence service again failed catastrophically. On 19 and 20 November 1942, two Soviet attacks broke through the brittle and overstretched German lines in the icy steppe to the north and south of Stalingrad. Those posts were manned above all by the Germans' allies; badly led, miserably equipped, and simply unequal to the task, they had little to set against the advancing Soviet tank wedges. The inevitable happened. By 22 November, the German Sixth Army was locked in; 200,000 men sat in the trap, in an enormous ruin surrounded by a frozen waste and by seven Soviet armies; 25,000 German soldiers were flown out of the encirclement, 110,000 went into Soviet captivity, only 5,000 returned to Germany. 'This is the last letter that I'll be able to send you,' wrote one German corporal. 'We've just been unlucky this time. If these lines are at home, then your son isn't here any more, I mean, on this earth...'. On 2 February 1943, the last German units capitulated. 'Temperature thirty-one degrees below, fog and red haze over Stalingrad. Weather station signing off. Regards to the homeland,' was the last German radio signal the *Wehrmacht* received from Stalingrad.

Despite all the drama, despite all the consequences, this was not *the* turn of the tide for the Second World War as a whole. The overall reversal of fortunes, which had already begun in the winter of 1941–2 and which can be tracked particularly closely on the Eastern Front, was, rather, a dynamic process. The Soviet odds of victory shortened as the German odds lengthened. Nevertheless, many

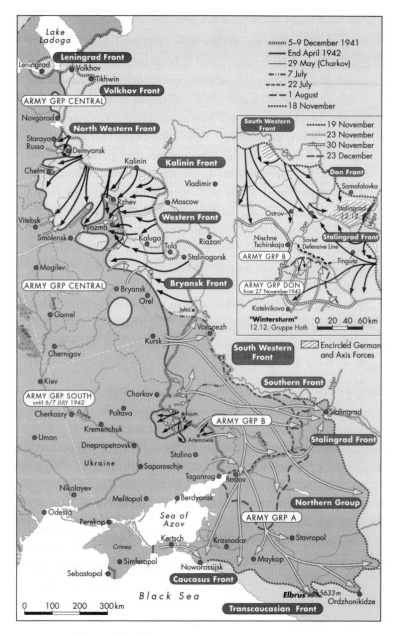

MAP 3. The Eastern Front in 1942

contemporaries felt that the battle for Stalingrad was the turning point of the war, because the slow, torturous, and ultimately pointless extinction of the entire Sixth Army took on a tremendously powerful symbolic value. According to a secret service report, the Germans were 'profoundly disturbed'. Germany's partners began to reconsider their role, and hope grew for the Allies. At that point, the Greater German Reich still held sway over almost all of Europe, at least on the map. The northern and central sections of the Eastern Front, where a grinding but inconclusive war of attrition was being waged, still seemed comparatively secure. But in the south there now yawned an enormous gap that threatened to widen ever further, and nor was that the only crack in 'Fortress Europe'. Around the Mediterranean, the Allies had succeeded in doing precisely what the Germans had tried to prevent: they had launched a Western offensive. The British had won at El Alamein (23 October to 4 November 1942), and Allied troops had landed in Morocco and Algeria (7–8 November 1942). All at once, the collapse of the German empire seemed close at hand.

The war from below: soldiers and civilians

Every war demands blood, sweat, and tears from its participants. To bear that in mind is anything but banal—it is, if nothing else, a moral necessity. Moreover, that reflection gives an idea of the conditions under which war is actually fought. Nevertheless, like every military undertaking, the German–Soviet War had its own unique characteristics—its extreme radicalization, for instance, which was something felt first by those at the bottom of the military pyramid.

Given the extent to which the war was shaped by wider factors such as the landscape and the weather, it was by no means rare for the experiences of the German troops to resemble those of the Soviets. Their letters, diaries, and memoirs habitually circle around a few central subjects: the unimaginable strain of war, but also the anecdotes derived from it; the exhilaration of battle, of victory, and adventure; the deeply felt comradeship that allowed them to endure more than seems possible; the humiliations at the hands of the military apparatus, but also its protective function; the killing and being killed; the loss of close friends and the resultant guilt; and finally apathy, despair, and naked fear. In these conditions, the soldier's life was concentrated for long stretches of time solely on surviving the day or on the microcosm of his unit. Everything else seemed secondary by comparison. For that reason if no other, soldiers had no sense of 'the big picture' and knew little or nothing about what their Commanders-in-Chief really wanted. 'We only see our little section of the front,' wrote a lance-corporal in January 1943, 'and don't know what's being planned on a larger scale'.

That is not to say that the deployment of these soldiers was without political implications or that they were indifferent to the military, political, and ideological superstructure of the war. On both sides, it was not unusual to fight with an extraordinary, almost religious devotion, not least because both believed themselves to have right on their side. On one side: the propaganda lie of a preventative strike; on the other: an appeal for unconditional dedication in the defence of the homeland. A Soviet recruit in January 1943 revealed that he had 'only a single thought: to become a marksman and destroy the fascists as quickly as possible, so that we can live happy and free again and see our dear mothers, sisters and girlfriends'. There is what reads almost like a direct response in a letter sent home from the Eastern Front in November 1944 by a young German Red Cross nurse: the war would be lost 'only in the moment in which we lay down our weapons. As long as a corner of Germany is still free of the enemy, I will not believe that history has sentenced my people to death.'

But nothing could be less accurate than explaining the position the soldiers were in and the actions they took solely with regard to their personal convictions. These were overwhelmingly determined by something else. Dirty, obedient, and overstrained, the troops felt hopelessly at the mercy of the war and of a vast system of labour division that was built on orders and submission, for which nothing counted but military rationale. It is unquestionable that individuals also had a degree of personal responsibility within this system. Sometimes this responsibility was large—as a result of a situation, of a mission, or simply because of their military rank. But it was far more common that individuals had little opportunity to voice their opinions or to take decisions. Most soldiers were in subaltern posts or performing subaltern functions, and their responsibility for what occurred remained correspondingly limited. It was this context that shaped their thinking and their actions more than anything else.

Contrary to widely held opinion, neither fighting nor war crimes were constant on the Eastern Front. The soldiers' everyday life was characterized by comparatively uneventful experiences: endless transports or marches; digging into positions or searching for something to eat, for somewhere to rest, or for a little privacy; keeping watch at distant posts; receiving orders; going on trips to the field hospital or even just waiting around for something to happen. This was then repeatedly interrupted by phases of drama and intensity in which much could be decided in the briefest time—one's own fate, that of the enemy, and also that of the civilian population. In fact, the military events proper were relatively unlikely to result in war crimes. Although battle was dynamic and necessarily characterized by both contact with the Soviets and a destabilizing unpredictability that could potentially lead to war crimes, these operations were nevertheless focused on engagement with a military enemy, and so the violence at least possessed a certain symmetry and equality. During periods of fighting, the individual soldiers were also borne by forces beyond their control. The situation was quite different once the battle had moved on; it was then that individual responsibility came to the fore. It is no coincidence that most of the crimes committed during the war took place far behind the front line.

These were not the only similarities in the daily existences of the German *Landsers* and the Red Army troops. Both learnt a new toughness and a huge capacity for suffering, another reason why they gave so little ground in battle. Both armies also bore an enormous weight of expectation from their supreme political and military commanders, whose all-too-often amateurish leadership did precious little to offset. Typical of the *Wehrmacht* as of the Red Army was a close consensus between the front and homeland, as was a fear of the enemy that made it impossible for many soldiers to imagine 'opting out' of the war. Indeed, desertion or captivity brought with them the grave dangers of being caught between two totalitarian dictatorships. Prisoners of war often ended up in places with a striking similarity to concentration or even death camps.

Of course, there were differences as well as similarities between the two sets of troops. Their behaviour bears the imprint of the different systems under which they operated. One cause of the

Germans' initial military success was surely the fact that the German soldiers, at least when it came to military tasks, were accorded a relatively high degree of autonomy. The bleaker the outlook became, however, the more extensive became Hitler's mania for control. In the Red Army, an opposite development can be traced, eventually resulting in what was almost an emancipation of the troops. *Almost*, because, on the whole, the Soviet Union handled its soldiers with an unimaginable indifference to human life; no army 'liquidated' so many of its own troops as the Red Army. When it comes to the war crimes of the *Wehrmacht* and the Red Army, there, too, the differences weigh more heavily than the undoubted similarities, something rapidly borne out by a closer analysis of the mentalities and reasoning behind these crimes, as well as of their scale. Finally, the two sides' military positions developed in opposite directions. While the German soldiers' lot continually worsened, the overwhelming experience of victory ameliorated some, though certainly not all, of what their Soviet opponents suffered.

At the end of the day, those who took part in this war did, after all, have one thing in common: those who survived the war would never forget it.

5

The German Occupation

Organization

The plan of constructing a German empire on the territory of the defeated Soviet Union was criminal and inhumane, not to mention very hard to accomplish. Alongside the invading armies proper, countless security and administrative personnel were required, as well as various specialists and also the kind of people who were not bothered by what the Reich Ministry for the Occupied Eastern Territories called 'scrapping the racially undesirable elements of the population'. At the beginning of the German occupation in the East, a whole range of large-scale organizations was founded, each with its allotted (supposedly complementary) role within the wider panoply of organizations. This division of labour was, as in the Holocaust, a crucial characteristic of the German occupiers' governance. In the vast operations undertaken to murder the populace, above all, this structure gave the perpetrators the psychological illusion that they were responsible 'only' for small sections, never for the whole.

From a bird's-eye perspective, the conquest of the Soviet Union by the German Reich resembles, as it were, an enormous process of digestion. At the front, at the extreme eastern edge of the area under German control, were the *Wehrmacht*'s combat troops, who, piece by piece, ate their way into enemy terrain with iron teeth. Behind them followed countless other units, military, semi-military, and non-military, whose task it was to digest the spoils as required by the strategy of the German invasion—that is, either to use, transform, or wholly discard them. Putting it like this may sound flippant but seems fitting nevertheless, because German rule was focused almost exclusively on the aims and interests of the occupiers. The further away one travelled from the fault lines of the war, the more distinct this enormous process of transformation and destruction became. In the areas further west, 'where the German Army's advances and combat operations lie further in the past', 'a widespread pacification among the populace is observable, something that was less developed further east and least developed in the area where the German armies are currently deployed', reported Task Force B in December 1941, albeit leaving open what it meant by the ambiguous term 'pacification'.

The relegation of the military literally to the edge of the German zone of control was necessitated by the logic of a war that did not go according to expectations. But it was also because the Nazi leadership did not really trust the *Wehrmacht* politically. As early as March 1941, Hitler had therefore ordered that the 'area in which the Army operates, as regards the hinterland, is to be restricted as much as possible', since the generals 'don't understand much about politics'. In the campaign against the Soviet Union, the Armed Forces were supposed to concentrate on the

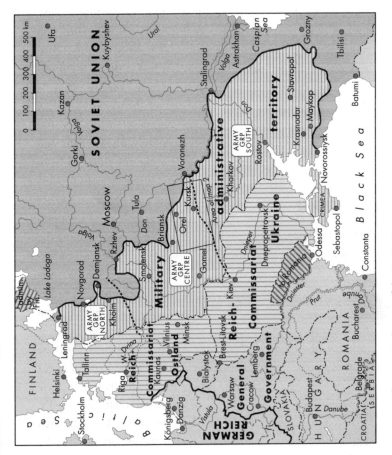

MAP 4. The occupied areas of the Soviet Union, autumn 1942

core of military activity, on 'the art of war'—and even there they were progressively to lose their autonomy.

The *Wehrmacht*'s traditional function as an army of occupation was starkly reduced from the very first. This happened partly through the founding of the Reich Commissariats, which began to be successively separated out from the area under military administration as early as July 1941. Also, however, in the zone that remained under the *Wehrmacht*'s control, it was no longer the master of its own house. Instead, it had to share the occupation of the Soviet Union with three other competing authorities: the SS, the organization charged with implementing the Four Year Plan, and the Reich Ministry for the Occupied Eastern Territories. The remits of these wholly different organizations were summed up by an officer of the General Staff as '*Wehrmacht*: defeating the enemy; Reichsführer SS: political and police struggle against the enemy; Reichsmarschall [Göring]: economy; Rosenberg: polit[ical] reconstruction'.

In theory, that sounded all very precise and efficient. In reality, however, the rivalries and turf wars of these four authorities, as well as their well-developed mutual jealousy, soon tangled the question of jurisdiction into a knot of commanders, borders, and privileges. This resulted not only in power struggles and a concomitant waste of energy, but also in an administration whose actions could be wildly heterogeneous. 'They happily go on governing any old how, usually one against the other, without any clear line predominating' was the opinion of such a well-informed contemporary as the Reich's Propaganda Minister, Joseph Goebbels.

The weakest was undoubtedly the civil administration—that is, the representatives of the Reich Ministry for the Occupied Eastern Territories. As the official 'bearers of the Reich's authority', they governed the two Reich Commissariats Ostland and Ukraine, which had been swiftly set up in the western part of the occupied Soviet areas. In summer 1942, these covered around a million square kilometres, around half of the German territorial gains. They were subdivided into General and Area Commissariats; the practical end of the hierarchy consisted of the 'indigenous administrators', principally mayors, who were usually there simply to carry out the wishes of their German superiors. These 'golden pheasants', as the functionaries of the civil administration were nicknamed because of their light-brown uniforms, were little respected and less loved. As one contemporary reported, they lived 'in the great expanses of the East, with uniforms and titles that were initially considered prestigious, with salaries, expenses and appropriations, puffed up with misunderstood slogans about their own mastery and the inferiority of foreign races' and tried 'to make up with a revolver and a whip or by an equivalent demeanour' for what they lacked in experience, ability, and authority. A 'German India' was what people of this type were supposed to create in the Soviet Union—that, at least, was the vision of the Nazi ideologues. But that was never really possible, if only because of the inadequate numbers of those employed in this role, to say nothing of other deficiencies.

Instead, it was Himmler's SS and police apparatus that soon became the *de facto* executive of the German occupation. In this instance, being the executive also meant that this organization had the most war crimes to answer for, by some considerable distance, in the civilian as well as in the military parts of the German occupied zone, something that reveals a lot about the institutional mentality of these men, even if they were thoroughly diverse as individuals. They were coordinated on the ground by the higher

SS and police leaders. The agency they directed was relatively small but highly compartmentalized: four 'Task Forces' (*Einsatzgruppen*, divided into *Einsatz-* and *Sonderkommandos*), around two or three dozen battalions of the 'Security Police', three brigades of the Waffen-SS, and, finally, the locally recruited Auxiliary Police. The core of these death squads was undoubtedly the Task Forces, which were constituted as microcosms of the Reich Main Security Office (*Reichssicherheitshauptamt*), the headquarters of the SS and the police. They were to follow hard on the heels of the *Wehrmacht*'s advance, and they played a key role in the Holocaust. It was usually only after they had passed through that the police battalions were deployed, which is why the latter were described as 'the rank and file of the Final Solution'. Meanwhile, the areas that lay between the routes along which the Task Forces advanced were combed through by brigades of the Waffen-SS. Since the strength of all four Task Forces combined was merely 3,500 men and that of the police battalions and Waffen-SS brigades around 30,000, this element of the German occupation's structure was particularly dependent on local assistance; by the end of 1942, the strength of the Auxiliary Police lay at around 300,000 men.

The body responsible for the 'entire economy' of the occupied Soviet Union, as defined by a protocol issued by the *Führer* in April 1941, was the 'Economic Organization East' (*Wirtschaftsorganisation Ost*) that Göring had called into being a few weeks beforehand. It was represented in the area under military control by a total of almost 20,000 specialists whose task it was to 'secure' the economic assets that the armies had conquered. Of that, as we shall see, there was no small amount. Within the Reich Commissariats, however, others were responsible: the economic specialists of the civilian administration, military armament inspectors, and, finally, the representatives of quangos called 'Eastern Societies', which used trustees and 'commissariat company directors' to take possession of those specific sectors of the Soviet economy that were of interest to them.

These were by no means the only organizations one would have encountered in the occupied zone. Almost the full institutional spectrum of the Third Reich was gathered there: *Organisation Todt (OT)*, the Reich Labour Service *(RAD)*, the National Socialist Motor Corps *(NSKK)*, the National Railway and the National Post as well as the German Red Cross *(DRK)*. Even the National Socialist Welfare Organisation *(NSV)* was there, as was the National Socialist Women's League in the form of nurses or 'settlement advisers', and finally also the Foreign Office, which sent 'representatives' and a 'special unit' to hunt down cultural loot. This conglomerate of authorities and institutions, whose personnel was equivalent to around 9 per cent of the field army, was supposed to build the New Reich in the East.

The other half of the German occupied zone, an additional million square kilometres inhabited by around thirty million civilians (in autumn 1942), was the responsibility of the *Wehrmacht*, although that, too, had initially never been intended. As a result, the *Wehrmacht*'s significance in the politics of the German occupation remained considerable. The territory under its control, which stretched eastwards from the Reich Commissariats, was divided into three broad strips, with the widest in the west and the narrowest in the east. By far the most troops were gathered in the war zone proper, which was in a sense the outer edge of the German empire. It was rarely more than 15 or 20 kilometres wide. It was, however, very long, a thin line of emplacements, trenches, and dugouts that in 1942 stretched 3,000 kilometres through the Soviet

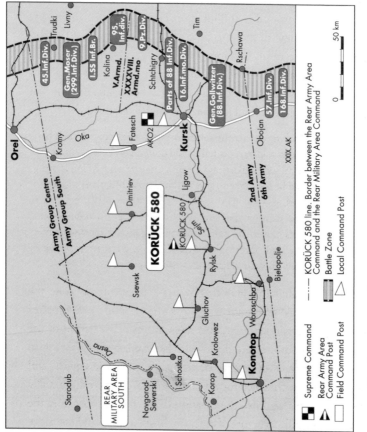

MAP 5. The German Second Army's sector of the Eastern Front and its rear area, May 1942

Union, from the primeval Finnish forests all the way down to the Black Sea. Since it was here, on the periphery of the German area of control, that the military struggle would be decided, around 75 per cent of all German soldiers were massed at the front; in 1942, that was around 2.1 million men. From a distance, there were astonishingly few of them to be seen. The emptiness of the battlefield was the result of a long historical development: new tactics, an increase in firepower, and the development of a new mobility had spread the soldiers ever further apart. But the war had not gone away, it had just become invisible:

> Someone looking across the terrain from a low-flying aircraft [a German Panzer soldier reported] could quite easily believe himself to be above an unpopulated wasteland. Only when looking more closely would he see the sentries standing in the irregularly zigzagging trenches, pressed hard against the sandbag walls, helmets down on the nape of their necks and binoculars to their eyes. Countless sets of eyes are constantly peering almost motionlessly across to the dark forest edge around 400 metres away, where white mounds of earth indicate the enemy's position.

Behind the main battle lines there was a kind of support zone, the 'rear *army* areas' (*Rückwärtige Armeegebiete*), around 50 kilometres deep, in which another 520,000 men, around 20 per cent of the military manpower, were deployed. They were responsible for an enormous arsenal of reserve or repair units, vehicle depots, and supply stores with which the divisions at the front were continually restocked. This was also the position of the field airports and the whole social infrastructure of the front: hospitals, the soldiers' mess, de-lousing and bathing facilities, cinemas, and much more. It was here that a soldier temporarily released from the war would encounter the first outposts of 'civilization'. Behind these—moving further west and now entering, in a sense, the third and last strip of the area administered by the military—were the 'rear *military* areas' (*Rückwärtige Heeresgebiete*). This was the lion's share of the territory under military control, and its size of between 100,000 and 150,000 square kilometres stood in an apparently almost inverse relationship to the number of soldiers stationed there, who never came to more than 100,000 *in total*. They were distributed across the thin network of field and local command posts, and allocated to the few Security Divisions who were actually to control this vast expanse.

All these organizations differed not only in their uniforms, but also in their troop strengths, their equipment and attitudes, their zones of operation and deployment, and last but not least their function. In Himmler's apparatus were concentrated all the most convinced Nazis and the enthusiastic anti-Semites, whereas a mass organization like the *Wehrmacht* provided a fairly accurate likeness of German society. That national, nationalist, or National Socialist attitudes dominated can hardly come as a surprise, and

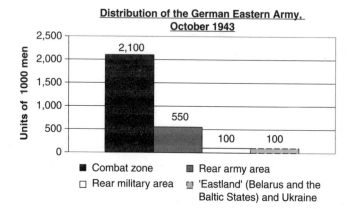

FIGURE 1. The distribution of the German army in the East

yet it was only nine years previously that, in the last free elections, no more than a third of the German electorate had voted for the NSDAP. Of course, much had happened since then. The regime's ability to create cohesion could be very powerful. But it is also true that the comparatively short Nazi period did not simply extinguish all other ways of looking at the world. Instead, it often merely hid or twisted them.

However, in this case, differences between individuals were certainly outweighed by the differences between institutions. In organizations such as these, an individual's behaviour was determined most strongly by the collective or by the superiors who were giving the commands. That applies equally to the much-debated question of involvement in war crimes and crimes against humanity. It should go without saying that all of those who participated (or, in the majority of cases, had to participate) in an undertaking that one of the masterminds of the German resistance described as 'a single enormous crime' were in some way responsible for it. However, there is a crucial difference between collective, institutional, and individual responsibility, and the last of these was highly variable. That applies particularly to the *Wehrmacht* with its millions of members. For example, an officer of the General Staff recounted how he and his commander had introduced 'all conceivable measures involving military police and tribunals' in an attempt to prevent looting in the zone they controlled. The same officer was forced to admit shortly afterwards that the Russians living there claimed 'never to have experienced a troop like ours'. These two observations demonstrate clearly the extent to which the behaviour of a mass organization like the *Wehrmacht* could vary. That is not to say that there were no differences of a structural nature in the attitude, organization, and functions of the German occupation. No one was more aware of that than the population on the ground. After 1945, Harvard University surveyed 1,000 Soviet emigrants to ask which of the Germans had in their opinion behaved in the best manner; 545 named the German combat troops, 162 the civil administration, and 69 the troops in the rear areas; the SS and the Security Police were chosen by just 10.

This heterogeneous apparatus of occupation had penetrated deep into Soviet territory. The Germans had conquered the most important regions of the USSR. This was where 40 per cent of the Soviet populace had originally lived; this was where 45 per cent of the grain was harvested, 60 per cent of the steel produced, and 65 per cent of the coal mined. However, a focus on the structural weaknesses of the German administration and on the fleeting and intermittent nature of its presence should by no means lead us to overlook the fact that this brief time was one of the harshest periods in the long history of this country and its inhabitants.

Between collaboration and resistance: Soviet society under the occupation

Between fifty-five million and sixty-five million Soviet citizens experienced German occupation—that is, around a third of the USSR's inhabitants. For many, it became the bitterest time of their lives, marked by the horrors of war, and of hunger, cold, forced labour, separation from loved ones, flight from their homes, displacement, and death. As if that were not enough, they were threatened by more than one enemy. The years of German occupation were only an interlude in a continuing Stalinist dictatorship that

ILLUSTRATION 5. One of the many millions of Soviet victims

attempted to use agents and partisans to control even those areas that were under German government.

Such conditions drove society into a state of near paralysis in which all remaining energies had to be expended solely on somehow surviving the war. Before 1941, Soviet society had lived carefully screened off from the rest of the world. Little was known about the Germans, and their invasion might as well have dropped out of the sky. Everything was made more difficult because the local administration disappeared upon the invaders' arrival. Soviet officials had fled, been imprisoned or shot by the Germans, or, most commonly, been moved further east. It is estimated that the Soviet side managed to transport between seven and a half million and ten million people away from the German advance—not just the majority of the state and party officials, but also that of party members and skilled workers. Another group of between six and a half million and nine million people fled of their own initiative. It was an enormous human wave that the German offensive pushed along before it. And another demographic vanished: able-bodied men. One often met only women, children, and the elderly. The German Third Panzer Army, for example, reported that the area under its occupation contained 20 per cent men, 30 per cent women, and 50 per cent children. These ratios alone indicate how hard it would be for them to survive.

What was certainly even worse was that the German leadership wanted nothing to do with the duty of care that law and custom prescribed. Instead, the German planners saw the occupied population as a series of problems, whether of security, supply, or disease. According to the principles of German racial doctrine, only very few ethnicities deserved humane treatment—that is, the ethnic Germans, the Estonians, and the people of the Caucasus. All others were regarded only as a potential resource for German interests, whereby the Ukrainians, Belorussians, and Latvians slightly outranked the Russians in this mad racist hierarchy. Right at the bottom were, of course, the Jews and the 'gypsies'; for them, there would be no room in the new German empire.

This biological conceptualization of what was in reality defined ethnically or socially, by religion or nation, was enough to decide the fate of many. Nevertheless, those who made a clear choice for one side or the other—whether by collaboration or by fleeing into the woods, to the partisans—remained in the minority. Most wanted, as human nature usually demands, to wait and see. At first, the German invasion had aroused hopeful expectation, partly because people remembered very clearly how it had been beforehand: the Bolshevik terror, the scanty food supplies, and, also, the comparatively moderate German occupation during the First World War. There were high hopes that private property would be returned to its former owners, that there would be a reorganization of agriculture, that there would be national self-determination and freedom of religion—hopes that the German occupiers fulfilled only rudimentarily or, in most cases, not at all.

The draconian orders given by the German High Command were not, however, always carried out in the way that it imagined. As their constant warnings and threats show, the troops sometimes modified or even ignored their instructions—at least in those instances where their room to manoeuvre was not obstructed from the outset by military necessity or by doctrine. In general, the daily reality of occupation has to be imagined as far more many sided than the German leadership's ideas would lead us to suspect; the temporal, spatial, and not least institutional differences were substantial. The spectrum stretched from blunt massacre to relations that were equivalent to those developed in the occupied areas of the First World War. The troops were in many ways dependent on civilian support—on cooks, seamstresses, cleaners, labourers for the roads, construction workers for defences, and many more besides. Early on, in September 1941, a German sergeant remarked that it was downright 'grotesque, how intimately' many German soldiers 'behaved with the Russians—contrary to all slogans—and how both sides derive an advantage from it'. By the end, however, all these differences would be levelled out, because the war was long, and the institutions, units, and people who exercised control were constantly changing. For those who had to endure it, that usually meant only one thing in the end: complete catastrophe.

The situation was worst in towns and cities. The Germans had conquered many large urban centres such as Riga and Vilnius, Minsk, Smolensk, Lviv, Kiev, Odessa, Kharkov, Stalino, Dnipropetrovsk, Rostov, and Sebastopol. Before 1941, a third of the Soviet population had been urban, but many towns had been emptied by the battles, as well as by flight, evacuation, and forced displacement. Many were now dominated by German garrisons—Smolensk, for example, where there were 50,000 German soldiers and only 37,000 indigenous inhabitants. Those who had remained in the towns were confronted with a series of almost insuperable difficulties, first among them that the battles were often focused on conurbations. It was also far harder to find supplies, they were more exposed to the interference or simply to the caprice of the occupying forces, and, lastly, it was the towns and cities that were the favoured victims of the 'scorched-earth' strategy, at the hands first of the Soviets, then of the Germans.

The majority of the indigenous population, of course, experienced the years of German occupation in the countryside rather than in the cities. At first, contact with the war and with the German conquerors was mostly short lived. But the effect of German occupation soon became ever more starkly visible. It began with administrative regulations, compulsory registration, restrictions on movement and transport, and limiting of the farmers' markets, all of which was followed by requisitions, taxes, relocations, forced labour, and even deportation to work camps in the Reich. Of even greater consequence was something quite different: the countryside was caught in the middle of a guerrilla war that hit the civilian population harder than anyone else.

Stateless spaces: the erosion of German power

It was in the expanses of the provinces that it was most obvious that the war was not going the way the Germans had expected. The conquerors had often done no more than drive through these parts of the Soviet Union. Their offensives had aimed above all at the military, administrative, and economic crux points of the giant Soviet empire, as well as at its few lines of communication. More was not possible for the *Wehrmacht*. Away from the towns, industrial centres, and roadways there thus existed vast spaces into which hardly a single German soldier ever wandered.

But a war could not be won like that, even in the hinterland. Truly to subjugate the occupied area, which was what the German leadership originally had in mind, the German security forces would have had to be far stronger than they were at a time when all units were needed at the front. Nevertheless, the German planners still held to their strategy of severity, exploitation, or destruction. Rather than consolidating or even rebuilding the occupied areas, most officials in the administration were interested in only one goal: ruthlessly fulfilling the requirements of supposed German interests, which were sometimes easily confused with personal ones. Although parts of the military administration and the ministerial bureaucracy had been advocating better treatment of the civilian population since spring 1942, and although that did sometimes come into effect on the ground, the nature of the regime and the war itself proved to be the deciding influences. The populace could not be palmed off with spirited speeches, services of thanksgiving, or amateur dramatics and folk-dance groups. Their hopes and expectations were soon bitterly disappointed, and, in consequence, the occupied area slipped ever further from its occupiers' grip. This process was strikingly described by a German participant in the war who would subsequently fall victim to it:

> We Westerners didn't understand these people or their country. Centuries separated us from their daily lives, their spirit and will…It was the borderless, the ungraspable and overwhelming aspect of this twilight country, that sent us back to our own borders…We took only riddles, interpretations and doubts home with us; our creeds and solutions were neither true nor useful. Thousands of words and statements failed to give a real picture of the place, and all that stayed true was the suffering we had experienced and witnessed during the war.

Nevertheless, it must be added that this war was not just about geography, anthropology, or culture; it was also always about ideology, politics, and economics, and the occupiers did almost nothing at all to win over the civilian population.

The development of the German 'living space' was correspondingly sluggish, and in fact it is hard to imagine a term that could have been less accurate. *Lebensraum* existed largely in the realm of wishful thinking and became a reality only in the lust for destruction that it caused. Settlers who would volunteer for this kind of suicide mission could hardly be found, and all that ever took shape were a few staging posts in the western Ukraine. Of the 4 Reich, 24 general, and more than 900 local commissariats originally planned, only half were ever formed and the rest of the occupied territory remained the strange hinterland of a war that refused to end. In other words: this inexhaustible country was hardly ever under the control of its occupiers.

Others quickly stepped in to take their place. The sheer size of the occupied territory and the nature of its terrain offered near-perfect conditions for a guerrilla war. From spring 1942 onwards, partisans began to spread ever more widely across the German occupied zone, and, only a year later, they controlled 90 per cent of the forests. Having grown up in the country and knowing it well, they found themselves in possession of an instant advantage. Yet more advantages were conferred by their strategy. It was a form of asymmetric warfare aptly summed up in the words of Henry Kissinger: the partisans win if they do not lose and the occupiers lose if they do not win.

During the course of 1942, the occupying German forces thus began to pull back ever further into a few core areas. The occupied towns were built up into fortified military bases while the rest of the German security forces were dotted like a pearl necklace along the main lines of communication, the roadways and the few central railway lines. Everything else became a no man's land, a kind of jungle where the strong ruled over the weak. That could be used by the occupiers—who now attempted to control their territory by laying waste or 'cleansing' whole landscapes in single operations—or indeed by the other side, the partisans. Only a small proportion of them were fighting on behalf of the Soviet state, which made the situation even more complex. It was the unprotected civilian population, however, that ended up in the crossfire between these various rival groups. At the moment in which the power of one regime had collapsed but the other had not really managed to replace it, a multitude of long-latent political, ethnic, or quite simply personal conflicts were free to erupt. It was almost a case of a *bellum omnium contra omnes*—a war of everyone against everyone, or otherwise of many overlapping and parallel civil wars. That was another reason why the zones occupied by the Germans were soon transformed into apocalyptic landscapes.

The inhabitants were thrown back on their own resources without the protection of laws or government. This has hardly ever been as hauntingly portrayed as in the film *Come and See*, in which the protagonist Flyora—like the famous German literary character Simplicius Simplicissimus before him in the Thirty Years' War—lurches through a world that has been thrown entirely out of kilter. That it was like this, that violence could become so normalized in the areas under German occupation, alters little when it comes to the responsibility of the occupiers. Their administration was dilettantish, parasitic, and destructive. In those circumstances, apocalypse was almost inevitable.

6

German War Crimes and Atrocities

It was during the war against the Soviet Union, if not before, that Nazism showed its true colours. In contrast to previous campaigns, all political, legal, or moral considerations that had previously been respected now fell away. Nazism revealed itself as a murderous utopianism—first for those it defined as enemies (and they were many), then for those who acted in its name (or for those on whose behalf it claimed to act). In this, the general picture of the war is misleading. Many German atrocities were not simply a result of chaos, hostile encounters, or a situation that had run out of control. Of course, that happened, too, but it was outweighed by what was planned, what was intentional. For example, the *Wehrmacht*'s High Command demanded of the troops, in an order prepared in May 1941—that is, before the beginning of the war—that they 'take uncompromising and energetic measures against Bolshevik agitators, partisans, saboteurs, and Jews, and eradicate all active or passive resistance'. Some of the other war crimes then took place because the invaders had created conditions in which they themselves then struggled to cope. In any case, this war of annihilation had a long prologue. It was rooted in stark ideological obsessions and also in strategic deliberations, some of which long pre-dated 22 June 1941. It is thus possible to discern a certain order amid the welter of human tragedy that the German occupiers left behind.

Jews

The invasion of the Soviet Union signalled the beginning of a new phase in the persecution of European Jews. Under the Nazi regime, they had until then been marginalized, humiliated, robbed, displaced, and even killed, but it was only now, after 22 June 1941, that the machinery of systematic murder was set in motion. The war not only offered Hitler the opportunity for—as he understood it—a definitive 'reckoning' with 'the Jewry'; it also allowed him to conceal methodical killing. It began early on. In a frenzy of violence on 27 June 1941, more than 2,000 Jews were slaughtered or burnt in the synagogue in Białystok. The perpetrators were German policemen. More common in these first days, however, were the bloody pogroms carried out primarily by the indigenous populations of the western Soviet territories, encouraged or initiated by Himmler's apparatus of Task Forces (*Einsatzgruppen*), police battalions, and the brigades of the Waffen-SS.

It was not long before this apparatus took personal control of the programme of murder. It was one of the central aims of the German occupation. As early as summer 1941, mass shooting followed mass shooting, claiming hundreds or sometimes even thousands of victims—officials, Romany gypsies, psychiatric patients, the 'politically unreliable', and 'Asiatics'. The largest group of victims, by a considerable margin, were the Jews, then 2.6 per cent of the Soviet population. The German death squadrons initially massacred the 'Jewish intelligentsia', then all Jewish men regardless of their occupation. From the end of July onwards, the German leadership was preparing 'a general solution to the Jewish question within the German sphere of influence in Europe', which meant in plain terms that now all Soviet Jews, increasingly also women and children, were marked out for the German policy of extermination. In the massacres that, in September 1941, were extended to entire Jewish communities, even the euphemisms gradually disappeared: 'Babies flew in great arcs through the air and we blasted them out of the sky before they could drop into the ditch or the water. Away with it, this brood that has plunged all of Europe into war...'. These were the words a police secretary from Vienna wrote home in October 1941. The largest bloodbath came on 29/30 September in the ravine of Babi Yar, where 'Special Unit' (*Sonderkommando*) 4a and two police battalions executed 33,771 Kiev Jews. 'During the night, I felt the cold body of my son underneath me and a mountain of corpses above that seemed to crush me,' remembered a young mother who managed to escape from the mass grave.

The genocide of the Soviet Jews had claimed almost 600,000 victims by March 1942. In the eastern part of the area occupied by the Germans, there were practically no Jewish people left. But it was after 1942 that most Jews would be killed. After 20 January 1942, the Wannsee Conference, all remaining European Jews became subject to a programme of extermination that had already become the norm in the occupied Soviet Union. Many Jews had thus far survived the German invasion, overwhelmingly in the western part, which was under civilian administration. A second wave of murders broke over these ghettos in spring 1942, taking the lives of another 1.5 million people by October 1943. Where, in

87

1941, male, able-bodied Jews had been the preferred victims, the German occupiers now tried to exploit them for as long as possible while all others were killed at once—from babies to the elderly. Seen overall, the German occupiers worked with a horrifying meticulousness: almost no Jews who came under their control in the Soviet Union were to survive it. The number of victims is estimated at around 2.4 million; of these, between 450,000 and 500,000 died in the area administered by the *Wehrmacht*.

For the army, there was no order to murder Jews. Nor did its commanders want it to. The guiding principle remained the division of responsibilities that had been agreed with the SS and the police, whose policy of murder was welcomed, tolerated, or resignedly accepted by *all* of the Eastern Army's High Command. The soldiers' attitude was similar; real resistance to the Holocaust was thinly sown. Nevertheless, relatively few soldiers *actively* participated in the genocide; those who did were in separate units operating mainly in the hinterland, where the distinction between partisans and Jews was increasingly ignored. If direct *individual* responsibility for the Holocaust was slight in the *Wehrmacht*, its *institutional* responsibility was immense. Without its administrative and logistical support, mass murder on this scale would never have been possible. It was the *Wehrmacht* that was first to organize the territories it occupied. That meant that its soldiers registered and marked the Jews, exploited them, and imprisoned them in the dozens of ghettos from which the SS and the police had only to come and get them.

There was also another source of outside help on which the murderers could rely. Alongside a not-inconsiderable number of anti-Semitic collaborators who appeared on the scene in the Baltic states, the former East Poland, and the Ukraine, the Romanian occupiers took on a particularly active role in the genocide. In Odessa alone, they killed at least 25,000 Jews at the end of October 1941 and, in total, they were responsible for the murders of 350,000 Jews in the south-west of the Soviet Union. But here, too, it must be emphasized that the initiative came from the Germans and that it was only as part of a project like Operation *Barbarossa* that a genocide of this character and dimension became possible.

Prisoners of war

This was the largest crime committed by the *Wehrmacht*: in their camps, around three million Soviet prisoners of war starved or froze to death, succumbed to epidemics, or were simply shot. Three million dead out of a total 5.7 million! That is, 53 per cent of all Soviet prisoners of war died while in the 'care' of the German military, most of them not in the chaos of a war zone, where danger, confusion, and crisis can cause things to escalate, but in camps that should instead have been characterized by safety and quiet. But the *Wehrmacht*'s guilt weighs more heavily even than this, because taking care of prisoners of war is actually a routine task for a professional army. On top of that, prisoners' rights had just been extended in international law, and this was ultimately a field in which the German military could act, on the whole, autonomously. This makes it all the more pressing to ask what caused this unprecedented war crime and, in particular, who bears the responsibility for it.

There was no especial indication before the outbreak of war that it would come to this, although there were certainly some signs that gave cause for concern. In March 1941, Hitler had let it be known in an internal discussion that the Soviet enemy, even

ILLUSTRATION 6. Soviet prisoners of war take a journey into captivity from which many of them would never return

after having been taken prisoner, was 'no comrade'. The central military organization subsequently issued standing orders in which it partly suspended the statutes of international law and also emphatically warned the German soldiers about 'treacherous Soviet wartime conduct'. What proved even more fateful was that the German network of POW camps—like so much else in Operation *Barbarossa*—was almost completely improvised. The number of camps—in 1941, there were eighty-one in the Soviet Union—was obviously inadequate. But can that really explain a crime of these proportions? After all, the prisoners were not supposed to die; they were supposed to work. In the German plans, it was this captured workforce that was to prevent the German war of manœuvre from grinding to a halt.

At first, 'only' two groups of prisoners were explicitly condemned to death by the German leadership: the political officers, the so-called commissars, and then, after autumn 1941, Soviet prisoners of Jewish origin. Around 50,000 of the latter lost their lives to the German 'screening', which was carried out by the Task Forces, by the police, or sometimes also by the *Wehrmacht* itself. Sometimes Soviet officers were shot at the same time, as well as 'Asiatics', women, and also, later, invalid prisoners, though these were not part of a systematic programme of murder.

The opposite was true for the commissars. Almost 5,000 were killed by the troops at the front, another 5,000 in the prisoner-of-war camps or the other rear areas. In places, the order to murder was construed by the army in even more wide-ranging terms than it was meant; in others, such an order led to discontent and criticism. From summer 1941 onwards, 'commanders, officers, and troops' repeatedly requested that the order be rescinded. Such a request was not normal. In the short history of the Third Reich, there are relatively few recorded instances in which criticism from below caused the political decision-makers to relent. This time, it was successful. On 6 May 1942, Hitler suspended the order regarding commissars—'on a trial basis', though it was never put back into effect.

These two groups of victims, however, represent only a small proportion of the total number of Soviet prisoners of war. Of the rest, most survived at first, at least until autumn 1941. Although there were killings while the prisoners were taken and also often during the torturously long marches to the prison camps, and although conditions upon arrival could be very tough, the differences between camps were still very large at that point. 'Everything is so peaceful, so well ordered,' a German sergeant was able to write about his transit camp in August 1941. But the tone of his letters home soon changed completely. 'This listless dying all around one is terrible,' he wrote in a letter from November. 'When they come to eat, stiff with frost—today it's minus ten, yesterday it was minus fifteen degrees during the day—they stagger, fall over, die at our feet.'

This constant, slow, and quiet dying soon became the norm in all 'Russian camps'. In autumn 1941, a series of problems all came to a head at the same time: the German offensive on Moscow had become bogged down, which went hand-in-hand with an acute crisis in the supply of the Eastern Army; the cold and wet time of year had begun; and the *Wehrmacht*'s victories in the 'cauldron' battles of Kiev, Vyazma, and Bryansk had brought another 1.5 million prisoners into the camp system. Since only half a million had been transported west to the Reich by the end of 1941, they bunched up in the zone of military operations. Of course, these were partly factors beyond any one person's control, albeit in a context created by the German High Command in the first place. What was more serious was their reaction to the crisis, in which all the amateurishness of their logistical planning came to the fore. Nothing better occurred to them than further to reduce the rations for Soviet prisoners in *all* camps, including those in the well-supplied West. The army's quartermaster-general made himself even clearer in a discussion on 13 November 1941: prisoners incapable of work—this was his monstrous order—were to starve. In the preceding months, the German leadership had already limited itself to doing only what was necessary for the Red Army soldiers and left the rest to the initiative of camp commanders. But now they were going to let the helpless prisoners of war die, the most vulnerable group in the conflict. The German camps soon transformed themselves into microcosms of hell: there were those who wept with hunger, those who ate the flesh of their dead comrades, those who begged the German guards to shoot them. Those who did not succumb to hunger succumbed to the cold or to disease, to dysentery, tuberculosis, or typhus. 'Like the Volga boatmen pulling their boats, around twenty prisoners pulled a wagon that was filled to over-flowing with naked corpses. Arms and feet hung over the edges,' a German sentry wrote in January 1942. By the time spring arrived, of the three million Soviet prisoners of war, only a third were still alive.

Those mainly guilty for their horrifying fate were doubtlessly those officials in the High Command of the *Wehrmacht* who were willing and able to accept that this would happen before it did. However, those further down the chain of command also bear their share of the guilt. In total, there were 245 'Russian camps' stretching the length and breadth of Eastern and Central Europe between the years 1941 and 1945. Those guarding them made up a tiny fraction of the total number of soldiers in the Eastern Army and as a result they bear a greater individual responsibility for what happened. There were camp commanders who were wholly indifferent to the plight of the prisoners or who even worsened their conditions. But there were also some who engaged themselves on the prisoners' behalf. The fact that this was barely possible after autumn 1941 shows how little freedom of action there was below the commanding heights of the military hierarchy.

Nonetheless, in spring 1942, it became clear in many camps that the German warders wanted to improve the prisoners' conditions. Particularly those prisoners who were prepared to work or even fight for the Germans benefited from it. However, the fact that by the end of the war another million Soviet prisoners had died in

German custody, many in the winter of 1942/3, shows just how limited the effect of these reforms would remain.

Partisans

Was it criminal for the German occupiers to fight a war against Soviet partisans? In principle, no. It is not a breach of international law if an occupying army mounts a defence against irregular aggressors, and it can also be militarily legitimate. In practice, however, things looked somewhat different. The war that the Germans waged against the Soviet Union was shaped in many ways by doctrine, and it was, above all, the civilian population that suffered the consequences. The occupiers were expected to take brutal action at the mere suspicion of disobedience or resistance. Hitler took this a step further. Very early on, on 16 July 1941, he explained frankly that the war against the partisans also offered certain advantages in that it gave 'us the opportunity to weed out what stands against us'. Here, too, the ideology of annihilation was the first priority, the army's security needs having been relegated to second place.

It turned out that the irregular Soviet troops were very tentative in finding their feet. The reaction to Stalin's call to arms, which declared a 'patriotic people's war against the fascist oppressor' in the first days after the invasion, was at first very modest. The majority of the officials, political agents, and other groups parachuted or otherwise smuggled in by the Soviet side were soon killed. The populace opted to wait and see. In the western parts of the Soviet Union, it was by no means rare for them to greet the *Wehrmacht* as liberators. For the *Wehrmacht*, the partisans were at that point far less of a problem than those soldiers who had been dispersed in all directions by the German encirclements of the Red

Army. These groups of survivors tried somehow to make their way back to their own lines because the Germans had warned that they would be classified as *francs-tireurs*, since they had failed voluntarily to present themselves for captivity at the correct time. This German threat was not only fraudulent, it was also plain stupid, and the consequences were not long in making themselves known. From autumn onwards, the attacks mounted behind the German lines. The *Wehrmacht* had always struck mercilessly when it saw its primary interests—security, scheduling, or supply—threatened, but executions of hostages or partisans were not yet the order of the day. That changed in autumn 1941. For example, the occupying 221st Security Division shot 1,847 'partisans' in only two months. *Suspicion* of being a partisan was now punishable by death, and the number of hostages also increased enormously. Field Marshal Keitel saw the deaths of '50–100 communists' as an appropriate 'atonement for the life of one German soldier'.

It could have been predicted that this terror would rebound on those responsible for it. That became the case after spring 1942. The partisan movement, now organized and led by a central staff in Moscow, began to take more robust shape. Entire partisan-controlled regions sealed themselves off behind the German lines and, on 5 September 1942, Stalin ordered that their war be made 'a matter for the whole people'—not just officials. This proved to be a successful policy: railway lines were sabotaged, bridges detonated, German outposts overrun, and collaborators murdered; in April 1943, 90 per cent of the vast Byelorussian and western Ukrainian forests were classified, from the German point of view, as 'partisan-infested'. In the summers of 1943 and 1944, the partisans' large-scale operations against the German lines of communication, the so-called railway war, had a direct influence on events at the front.

The German troops deployed there, depleted and losing their shape, already had more than enough on their hands just resisting the constant attacks of the Red Army. The partisans were supposed to be kept under control by the rearward forces—a militarily rather pitiful alliance of the *Wehrmacht*'s Security Divisions with police battalions, brigades of the Waffen-SS, indigenous troops and often also soldiers from Germany's allies. They compensated for their weakness with terror, as per Hitler's explicit instructions, and with what were euphemistically called 'major operations' (*Großunternehmen*), in which whole areas were surrounded, 'cleansed', and then reduced to ashes. These operations did not usually reach the partisans themselves, who moved on quickly and reassembled their forest encampments elsewhere. The main victims of this strategy were, instead, the civilians unfortunate enough to be living there. It is estimated that only between 20 per cent and 30 per cent of those killed were actually partisans. What remained behind were desert zones: desolate countryside, burnt-out villages, and piles of corpses. 'In partisan areas, women and children suspected of supplying the partisans with food are to be dispatched with a shot in the back of the neck,' one young soldier reported in a letter home from 1942. Between February 1942 and June 1944, there were no fewer than sixty-eight such 'major operations'. The casualties were as one would have expected, including with regard to their disproportionate nature. The Germans lost around 50,000 people in the partisan war, the Soviets ten times as many, around 500,000.

Of course, in this, too, the reality was more complex than the orders, structures and figures would suggest. The partisans were equally unwilling to give any quarter; whether to the enemy (whose soldiers were at first taken prisoner only rarely), to collaborators and their families, or to the ordinary civilian population, even those who did not want to be involved, from whom the partisans often extracted support and supplies by force. 'It was a hard life,' acknowledged a former Soviet partisan leader after the war. 'They [the Germans] were ruthless. And so were we.' This applied not only to these two sides. The underground movement in the occupied Soviet territories was far more heterogeneous than later Soviet historiography would have had us believe. Alongside 'red' groups, there existed also pro-Polish, Ukrainian, Baltic, and Jewish partisans, as well as those who simply wanted to survive outside the law. That all these groups were often sworn enemies of each other hardly simplified the situation.

There is, however, one more nuance to add. Although the *Wehrmacht* acted brutally towards partisans, whether real or suspected, it began also to experiment with another approach after 1942: offers of amnesty to partisans, differentiated treatment of civilians, economic reforms, and sometimes also careful proposals of military or political autonomy to collaborators, above all by the Commander-in-Chief of the Second Panzer Army, General Rudolf Schmidt. Experience teaches how extremely difficult it is to bring such experiments to fruition once the spiral of violence has already begun to turn. Within the parameters of the Nazi regime, however, they were doubly doomed to failure, and it was the Soviet underground that benefited. The area behind the lines eventually became a kind of second front capable of influencing the general military picture. This was a direct consequence of a German strategy that was equally criminal and myopic, in which the only possible peace was the deathly quiet of the grave.

Leningrad

Hitler attempted to make even the core business of the military, operational planning, directly subservient to his ideology of extermination. He was to manage this on only one occasion, but with devastating consequences, in the siege of Leningrad. The operation was not really militarily justifiable. The German leadership wilfully halted the advance of Army Group North in September 1941, so as to spare their strength and let the city's three million inhabitants starve to death. At that time, starving out a city was not prohibited as a tactic of war, but in this instance military planning was secondary to the motive of systematic genocide. Instead of deciding the war on this section of the front, disarming more than thirty Soviet divisions and securing an enormous staging post, military logic had to give way to Nazi ideology. The blame for setting this course lies primarily with Hitler, for whom Leningrad was a 'nest of snakes', a symbol of the Bolshevik Revolution; but the responsibility lies also with the military advisers who wanted to 'let Petersburg stew in its own juice', as Quartermaster-General Wagner jokingly put it. A staff officer with Army Group North subsequently wrote that there was 'no intention' of 'going into the city'; Leningrad was 'the birthplace of Bolshevism', and the city therefore had to 'disappear from the face of the earth, as Carthage once did'. This was the tone of the war games being dreamed up in the *Führer* HQ and the *Wehrmacht* High Command.

Those chosen to put this criminal approach to warfare into practice were the locally deployed 18th Army, an assignment of which most of its members were probably never aware. They were part of a large-scale operation that from the outside appeared military in nature. They were not party to their leaders' true intentions, and instead their task was explained as besieging and bombarding the city until the Russians surrendered. Internally, the Reich's propaganda minister, Goebbels, let it be freely known that the Soviet resistance was 'an effective alibi' for 'the terrible fate' that awaited the city. The soldiers at the front were not informed. And nor would they have wanted to be. In the files of the German military, one opinion continually recurs: that it would be unendurable for the soldiers stationed there if 'during each break-out they had to shoot at women and children and defenceless old men'. The soldiers of the 18th Army were spared this final escalation of ideological warfare; neither the city nor its inhabitants capitulated.

Leningrad was not actually supposed to remain a unique case. In July 1941, Hitler had declared that Moscow, too, would be 'razed to the ground' and its inhabitants wiped out by artillery and hunger; something similar was also planned for Stalingrad. That, at least, was prevented by the Red Army, but the city of Leningrad was condemned to a slow death by starvation. The city was wedged in between German positions to the south and Finnish troops to the north, where the Finns had advanced to the old Finno-Russian border and dug in. Between the two, as if on a small island, there remained a chunk of Soviet territory bitterly defended by soldiers and civilians whose existence narrowed until it consisted only of this struggle. And indeed, by late autumn of 1941, the *Wehrmacht* had missed its opportunity to conquer the metropolis on the Neva. The battles disintegrated into a hard, grinding siege, into a war of attrition around the city in which the energies of the two opponents were entirely used up in trying either to lift or to maintain that siege. By 18 January 1943, the Soviet Second Army had carved out a slim overland connection to the city, a few kilometres wide, to the south of Lake Ladoga. A year later, heavy Soviet attacks forced the German 18th Army to retreat in the direction of Estonia. Leningrad was free. The 'blockade' had lasted 880 days.

For those who did not manage to escape the trap, it was terrible. By October 1941, the number of dead in Leningrad exceeded the usual mortality rate by around 2,500; by November it was 5,000; by December it was nearly 50,000. From the perspective of an 11-year-old Leningrad schoolgirl, that meant:

> Shenja died on the 28th of December 1941 at 12:00 o'clock; grand-mother died on the 25th of January [1942] at three in the afternoon; Lyoka died on the 17th of March at five in the morning; Uncle Vasya died on the 13th of April two hours after midnight; Uncle Lyosha on the 10th of May at four in the afternoon; mother on the 13th of May at half past seven in the morning. The Savichevs have died. Everyone has died. Only Tanya is left.

Tanya Savicheva was unconscious when she was found. Her health badly damaged, she died on 1 July 1944 in a hospital out-side the city. Even when, after spring 1942, the situation gradually improved, even when supplies began to arrive over Lake Ladoga, by boat in summer and over the ice in winter, on the legendary 'road of life', even when Leningrad was increasingly evacuated and beginning to be transformed into a productive 'front city', people continued to die. The estimates of the number of those whose lives were claimed by the German siege range between 600,000 and 1,000,000 people.

As often happens in such conditions, the German strategy of starvation brought out the best and the worst in its victims, the *blokadniki*. One who was there wrote: 'At every turn there was infamy and nobility, self-sacrifice and egoism, theft and honesty.' And even then and there, the hunt for 'enemies of the people' went on. Unmoved by what was happening, the NKVD, the secret police, reported that they had 'arrested 9,574 people' and 'liquidated 625 counter-revolutionary groups' in Leningrad between June and September 1942. But this story's dark sides alter nothing about its outcome. It was a Soviet victory, almost immediately a military myth, a successful defence of a situation in which the defenders had been left with no alternative. And: it was a crime committed by the Germans, one of many, but nonetheless a crime that, even then, was unparalleled.

Economic exploitation

The consequences of German economic exploitation of the Soviet Union have long been underestimated, despite its having been visible everywhere. The policy of the German leadership, which was to rule and squeeze the East like an enormous colony, simultaneously pursued a number of aims, some of which were mutually contradictory. In the light of the scarcity of their own resources, they wanted the *Wehrmacht* to live 'wholly off the land', but, at the same time, the German home front was supposed to profit from the Soviet Union's harvests and natural resources. The ultimate goal was economic autarky—this with one eye on a final struggle against Britain and America. But the German planners were not concerned only with economics. Even before the launching of the campaign, they had, with staggering indifference, calculated on the death by starvation of the conquered populace, projecting that this would happen to 'x million people'. In short, economic blueprints here overlapped with those of genocide.

These projects—vast, complex, and also enticing—were not to be left in the hands of the common man. Spontaneous looting was to be met with 'the strictest punishment'. Those better equipped for the task were the experts of the Economic Organization East. They bear by far and away the greatest responsibility for the rapacious extortion that ensued. That they did not act alone did not improve matters for the occupied populace. The *Wehrmacht*'s quartermasters and supply divisions naturally wanted to provide for the units in their charge, and the Reich commissariats, too, sent 'economic experts' to extract whatever could be extracted. As if that were not enough, in spring 1942, Fritz Sauckel took the stage as General Plenipotentiary for Labour Deployment. By June 1944, his officials and henchmen had transported 2.8 million Soviet forced labourers into the German Reich as part of a programme that increasingly reminded witnesses of the slave hunts of times gone by. When the forced labourers arrived in the German Reich, their situation hardly improved, though it is true that those sent to work on farms were significantly better off than those others who worked in industry, in construction, or in the mines. A French prisoner of war compared his camp with one of the many 'Russian camps' and said of the latter that it was 'horribly overfilled, men, women and children herded together…the provisions usually inedible'.

In the occupied Soviet Union, the German troops eventually did what, depending on the situation, could be called requisitioning, administering, extraction, or simply plunder. 'The soldiers go into vegetable gardens and take everything,' wrote a company commander of the 384th Infantry Division. 'We threaten severe punishment, but the ordinary soldier hardly holds himself back. Hunger forces him to behave this way.' In a war that the German High Command had started with enough rations for only twenty days, that could have been predicted. 'Even in the most unexpected things (needles, oil, nails etc) we're in a state of need out of all proportion to the scale of our military program,' was the assessment of the Staff of the 251st Infantry Division. Because the German units were massed at the front, this plundering occurred above all in the battle zones and the area immediately behind, which was soon stripped as bare as if by locusts.

Nevertheless, the Economic Organization East did eventually succeed in supplying 80 per cent of the *Wehrmacht*'s needs from the occupied Eastern territories while simultaneously transporting goods back to Germany. What these uninvited but demanding guests required can be illustrated with the help of some figures. Army Group A alone consumed 187,000 cattle and 434,000 sheep in ten weeks. The German administration also kept meticulous records of everything that was transported into the Reich, of raw material, industrial products, foodstuffs, and even workers. Around 2 million tonnes of scrap steel had been sent back by March 1944, along with 1.1 million tonnes of iron ore, 660,000 tonnes of manganese ore, 14,000 tonnes of chromite, and so on. This list goes on and on until it finally ends with 12,000 tonnes of wool and more than 178,000 oxtails that were also required by the German war economy. In other words, it was a programme of looting such as the world has rarely witnessed.

There is more that remains hidden behind these figures. The Soviet populace had already often found itself forced to live in the harshest of conditions, even leaving aside the catastrophic famines of the previous decades. Now it again became the victim of a policy of starvation. They were to be fed, if at all, with the absolute bare minimum. Up to the winter of 1941/2, the ration shrank continuously. For the non-working urban population, that meant 70gr of fat per week, 1.5kg of bread, and 2kg of potatoes. Those who collaborated or worked for the *Wehrmacht* were slightly better off. There were also substantial regional differences, but, in total, around half of all the Soviet civilians under German occupation went hungry. Hit especially hard were the German-occupied hinterland around Leningrad, the Donets Basin, the north-eastern Ukraine, the Crimea, and the towns and cities. In May 1942, 40 people starved to death every day in Kharkov; by the end of 1942, 14,000 people had died of hunger there. When a German medic noticed 'children and old women' who 'consisted literally of skin and bone', it was not the result of some kind of state of emergency. It was the result of a policy on which people like Herbert Backe, then State Secretary in the Reich Ministry for Nutrition and Agriculture, had decided even before the outbreak of war: 'The Russian has borne poverty, hunger and frugality for centuries. His stomach is elastic, so no misplaced pity.'

That it did not become even worse was because at least a proportion of the troops supplied provisions to their civilian neighbours, something their superiors criticized as 'misconceived humanitarianism'. From 1942 onwards, other voices began to be heard: the 11th Army, for example, demanded that the civilian population 'be fed as a whole...regardless of whether they work for us or not'. Alongside humanitarian, political, and propagandist motives, economic considerations also had a role to play. After February 1943, all civilians stood under a general obligation to work, for example, on the construction of roads or military positions or in the local factories that were now supposed to be run rather than stripped. This heightened exploitation, however, often more than outweighed the tentative improvements in food provision. Although the catastrophic starvation winter of 1941/2 was not repeated, the civilian population remained firmly at the bottom of the German quartermasters' scale of priorities. The number of those who starved to death reached into the hundreds of thousands, if not the millions.

Scorched earth

Although the war that the Germans brought to the Soviet Union had already inflicted innumerable wounds on it, the occupiers' violence reached another peak when they were forced to leave their 'living space'. Never had they so systematically destroyed and depopulated the country.

The concept was not new. There had already been scorched earth in many other wars, but it was surely no coincidence that this form of warfare was present in the Hitler–Stalin war right from the start. It was the Soviet side that first made use of the strategy. Everything that could not be transported—factories, roadworks, stores of raw materials—was to be ruined. Stalin wanted to create 'unbearable conditions' for 'the enemy and all who help him'. The more the German advance slowed, the more that did indeed become the case. It must be said in the Soviets' defence, however, that their priority was to evacuate rather than to wreck, that they were doing it in their own country, and that they had not started the war in the first place. On top of that, this partial self-destruction was a strategy with high hopes of success. After all, the Russians had already used scorched earth in 1812 to sap the strength of Napoleon's *Grande Armée*.

When the Germans began their own work of devastation and turned the countryside into wasteland, the prospects were different. The more hopeless their military position became, the more radical were the orders issued from the High Command, although it was easy to see by 1943/4, at the very latest, that these measures no longer had any military justification, to say nothing of any moral or legal defensibility. At heart it was now only a programme of collective suicide. Hitler and his accomplices wanted to take as many with them as they could on their march into the *Götterdämmerung*.

During the first retreats in the dramatic winter months of 1941/2, the *Wehrmacht* had already left areas of desolation behind. 'The night was lit blood-red by the villages burning around us', wrote one German soldier, 'and from the dark hills resounded the thunder of detonations.' At that point, the destruction was still confined to relatively restricted areas, but there were already soldiers and units whose opinion was that this was not 'commensurate with our perception of ourselves as a civilized people'. Moreover, at that point, it was not the main intention to inflict long-term economic damage on the enemy, but rather just somehow to keep him at a distance. This destruction was usually motivated by simple fear, but it was of little avail. 'How often did we think that the Russians would not be able to establish themselves in these burnt-out localities', complained a German infantryman, 'and then by the following morning they would be right behind us again.'

Compared with what the German occupiers did after the winter of 1942/3, this was all just a dry run. What had been a tactic became a strategy. Hitler demanded that 'the land that the enemy takes over must be lastingly and completely unusable, an uninhabitable desert where mines go on exploding for months'. A few months previously, in February 1943, he had already lambasted his generals because 'too little [had] been destroyed during the retreat'. It was something in which the German occupiers would soon have plenty of experience. Their procedure was systematized and perfected as LCJD: loosening, clearing, jamming, destroying. The area they had occupied sank ever deeper into rubble and ash. In the second half of the war in the East, the Germans left behind mile-wide firestorms, blown bridges, torn railway lines, poisoned wells, unusable factories, and ruined power plants, as well as prisons and camps, such as in Minsk, that were populated only by the dead. They began to take everything that could be carried—resources, goods, and increasingly also people.

The first large-scale deportations took place during the battle of Stalingrad, and by the spring of 1943 deportation had already become a system. Another 2.3 million Soviet civilians lost their homes and all of their possessions to it. They were used as workers in the Reich or locally by the German troops, or alternatively were driven off into the empty wastes. A part of this exhausted and terrified mass of people followed the retreating German columns more or less voluntarily, as some of the German reports noted. Fear of a return to life under the Stalinist regime was sometimes very strong. But their willingness to accompany the Germans to their downfall would only decline as the war continued. As a result, the Germans became ever more rigid in their efforts to keep and to exploit this potential workforce, which was needed, for example, for the increasingly urgent construction of defensive positions. But things were no better for those known in the German jargon as 'useless eaters'. It sometimes happened that the occupiers, after long and gruelling marches, drove the elderly, the infirm, the women, and children into internment camps, where they were left to await their fate. Eventually, those still alive were rescued by the advancing Red Army. Its soldiers then received a very precise idea of how things had been under the German occupation. That was one reason for the hate and bitterness that spread throughout the Red Army after the winter of 1941/2. 'I would not like to be taken prisoner in the next Russian offensive,' wrote a young German artillery officer, 'because I can more or less imagine what they will do to German prisoners after they have come through the areas we have emptied and the burnt-out villages and find the soldiers executed by the side of the road ...'.

The military does not bear sole responsibility for this awful finale to the German occupation. It was rather the case that here, too, the whole apparatus that the Germans had installed in their brief tenure in the Soviet Union now swung into action—countless civilian bureaucrats, the Economic Organization East, the Reich Labour Service, *Organisation Todt*, as well as those led by Sauckel, the General Plenipotentiary for Labour Deployment, and ultimately, of course, the combat troops themselves, who were inevitably the last to abandon their positions. It was not rare for the Eastern Army's retreats to be accompanied by a general feeling of apocalypse that could give way to a sense of 'devil take the hindmost'. At the end it was so bad that, according to one German general, 'every little baggage porter felt called upon to cause some destruction'. That is not to say that *all* soldiers behaved like this. Sometimes there was no willingness to do so and sometimes no time or opportunity, because organized, well-prepared retreats remained an exception. Nonetheless, photographs of liberated Soviet territories speak for themselves. One of those who would know, a specialist adviser to the German Military Administration, said that it was 'the most calamitous thing' he had yet experienced in the eastern campaign.

7

Politics 1941–1945

German foreign policy

'Politics? I'm not getting involved in any more politics. I find it so nauseating,' Hitler is supposed to have complained during a discussion of the situation in April 1945. It was far too late for that. He had initiated his departure from politics long before. Since 1939, with a remarkably suicidal consistency, he had burnt one bridge after another and so steadily reduced the number of paths that German diplomacy could take. Foreign policy soon consisted mainly of the *Wehrmacht*'s military successes. If there were none of those, as was the case from winter 1942–3 onwards, it soon became unavoidably apparent how completely the German Reich had become a prisoner of Hitler's ideological obsessions. That is not to say that German diplomacy came to a standstill in the second half of the war; a selective edition of the most important documents in German foreign policy from September 1941 to May 1945 still runs to eight thick volumes. But the Foreign Office had ceased to be a motive force long before and was now being driven along only by others. Its activity was gradually restricted to trying to plaster over the cracks in Hitler's Fortress Europe and hold it together by any means available, be they persuasion, pressure, or, if necessary, brute force.

But the one crucial signal never came. The German leadership never presented a serious proposal for ending the war, nor for a separate peace, be it with the Western powers or with the Soviet Union. That was despite having long known that the war was lost. In January 1943, at the latest, when the USA and Great Britain agreed at the Casablanca Conference (14 to 25 January 1943) not to accept less than unconditional surrender from the Axis of Germany, Italy, and Japan, the possibility of a compromise between Germany and the Soviet Union also became more difficult. This was because the message from Casablanca was addressed also to the Soviet partners, who had stayed away from the conference: there was no longer any question of a separate peace with the enemy. Stalin took his time in responding, using his order of the day to do so on 1 May 1943: the principle of 'unconditional surrender by Hitler's Germany' was now the point on which all the Allies' policy was oriented. Nevertheless, the idea of a separate German–Soviet peace floated around the High Commands of both sides in the first half of 1943 and then again in summer 1944. While Stalin, at least, never entirely dismissed the thought of a separate peace treaty with the hated enemy, it was always out of the question for Hitler. There was 'no line on which Germany and Russia ... would be able to agree', Hitler informed his ally Mussolini in December 1942, when the latter urgently counselled that they do just that. However, the *Führer* no longer had anything like a strategic alternative to offer. The hopes that sustained him were increasingly delusional: was it not possible that the unnatural Allied coalition would fall apart? Or that all fascist parties would unite to form a pan-European volunteer movement in the fight against Bolshevism?

International politics continued untouched by these daydreams, the only change being that it slid further out of German reach. The German war in the East had always depended on support from large parts of Europe, and mobilizing them became ever harder after 1943. When Italy brought its last troops home in April and May 1943 and when, in October, Spain recalled its volunteers, those who had fought in the 250th, the Blue Division, it showed which way the wind was blowing. And that was only the start. In late summer 1944, confronted with the news of overwhelming Soviet victories, the anti-Bolshevik front in Eastern Europe collapsed within a matter of weeks. The German Eastern Front lost its cornerstones when Romania and Finland switched sides in August and September, respectively; also in September, hitherto neutral Bulgaria went over definitively to the Soviet side. For Hungary, Slovakia, and Croatia, it was only the military situation that prevented them from leaving the Axis camp. The occupation of Hungary by German troops on 19 March 1944 and the crushing of the pro-Soviet uprising in Slovakia (October 1944) demonstrate how difficult it was becoming for the German leadership to keep these allies within the camp.

No political conclusions were drawn from these developments, right up to the end. Even on 29 April 1945, the day before his suicide, Hitler dictated in his 'political testament' that 'our goal must still be to win living space in the East for the German people'. That was all he had to offer. The problem was that German diplomacy went along with it. It never suggested any alternatives to the road that led to political and moral downfall, and, in fact, as a rule, never even took them into serious consideration. Since Hitler had inextricably nailed his personal fate and that of the nation to the outcome of the war, the Foreign Office degenerated to become the obedient servant of its *Führer*, turning Clausewitz's dictum on its head: politics became a continuation of war by other means. Rarely has the twisting of this maxim, which demanded the opposite, the consistent subordination of the military to the political, been carried to such extremes as it was in the German foreign policy of that period.

Soviet foreign policy

As German foreign policy appeared ever more leaden and unsuccessful on the international stage and the 'fascist belligerent alliance' came ever further apart, Soviet diplomacy became ever abler and more effective. That need not have been the case, since its starting position could hardly have been worse. On 22 June 1941, Soviet diplomacy had been more or less a heap of rubble. But there were more opportunities than was initially apparent. While Stalin had been left speechless at first and had needed almost two weeks before explaining to his 'brothers and sisters' over the radio why their German friends were now again to be their enemies, others found their voices far more swiftly. One of these was Winston Churchill. He was able to continue undeflected from his course, not least because a new set of potential allies had just appeared. As early as the evening of 22 June, he greeted the Soviet Union as a new partner to whom would be given 'whatever help we can', because 'the cause of any Russian' was 'the cause of free men and free peoples in every quarter of the globe'.

Churchill meant what he said. By the end of August 1941, the first British convoys reached Archangel and Murmansk via the 'northern route'; in September, British and Soviet troops occupied Persia so as to secure a supply route from the south; and, in November 1941, the first of an enormous quantity of American supplies arrived in Russia. The legendary 'lend-lease programme' had begun. The USA delivered goods with a total worth of some $10.8 billion to the Soviet Union, Great Britain adding another $5.9 billion worth. These figures are not the only things that speak for themselves. That the formality of corresponding mutual assistance pacts, between the USSR and the UK, and the USSR and the USA, were written and signed only much later (May and June 1942), also demonstrates the urgency with which the Western powers desired a military alliance with the Soviet Union.

Material aid was followed by ever more diplomatic concessions. This was always also an expression of guilty conscience, because for a long time the Western Allies were simply not in a position to comply with Stalin's demands and open a second front, something he first asked them for on 18th July 1941. Far more important was that the Western powers knew just how difficult it would be to win the war without the Soviet Union. That made them willing to accept much they would not have considered otherwise. For the Soviets, on the other hand, this was a unique opportunity to improve their standing in global politics. This improved standing was not something that could be taken for granted, as the isolation of the USSR in the 1920s and 1930s or its role in the descent to war amply suggest. But that now all seemed less important. The common enemy, Hitler, not only formed the basis of a 'strange' alliance, but also ultimately provided the 'victory over fascism' with which the USSR hauled itself up to the rank of superpower.

The legitimizing of its imperial power politics was ultimately also part of that process. As early as December 1941, when battles were raging on the approach to Moscow, Stalin requested that British Foreign Minister Anthony Eden recognize the Soviet borders as they had been on 22 June 1941. The long wait for the opening of the second European front that the Soviet Union had so passionately demanded soon developed into an ever greater diplomatic advantage. Great Britain was not capable of storming Fortress Europe by itself, and even such a powerful ally as the USA, which entered the calculations in December 1941, needed time to arm and prepare. That meant that it was the Soviet Union that had to bear the main burden of the war in Europe, but also that it could extend its sphere of influence to a great extent undisturbed, shape its far-sighted European policy to its own taste, and then finally also secure the centre of the German Reich as its own.

The Soviet wartime and post-war strategies were first carefully adumbrated at the Moscow Foreign Ministers' Conference (19 to 30 October 1943) and the first meeting of the 'Big Three' in Teheran (28 November to 1 December 1943). The military contribution that Stalin was then able to present to Churchill and the US President Franklin D. Roosevelt (1882–1945) was deeply impressive, and Churchill would not be deflected from ceremonially offering Stalin a gift of thanks from the British King George VI—the Sword of Stalingrad. By comparison, the military contributions of the Western Allies still looked modest, despite all efforts made and losses suffered. Despite their successes in North Africa and Italy, as well as on the seas and in the air, Western Europe was still largely in German hands. It seemed only right that Stalin would make demands, and this did not elicit any real resistance from his Western partners. No one wanted to risk a schism in the alliance at that point. Moreover, there were also issues on which the partners found themselves, then at least, in full agreement: that the Western Allies would make a landing in Western Europe, that Germany would be weakened and dismantled, that German war criminals would be tried, that Poland would be shifted west, that the USSR would join the war against Japan, that Tito would be recognized as Allied Commander-in-Chief in Yugoslavia, and that once the war was over world peace would be mutually secured. During the previous months, Stalin had moved to please his new Western comrades where it cost him little; for example, the USSR's signing of the Atlantic Charter (24 September 1941), the Declaration by United Nations (1 January 1942), the dissolution of the Communist International (15 May 1943), or the reception of the Russian Orthodox Church's representatives by Stalin (4 September 1943) and the election, three days later, of the first Moscow Patriarch since 1917.

The Big Three were to meet once more during the war, this time in Yalta (4 to 12 February 1945). At that point, Stalin was occupied with hastily Sovietizing Eastern and South-Eastern Europe in order to create *faits accomplis*. It was also evident from this that the Soviet Union would definitely retain the territorial gains made through the Hitler–Stalin Pact and indeed extend them at the expense of Germany and Finland (as well as Japan). Stalin, playing the consummate host in this former holiday resort, knew precisely what it was he wanted. The terminally ill Roosevelt did not want to endanger his legacy of a new world order, nor relinquish the possible entry of the Soviet Union into the war against Japan. That isolated Churchill, who showed himself almost too receptive to the overabundant Soviet hospitality. The three-way summit eventually confirmed what was already marking itself out on the map—namely, the imperial annexation of Eastern Europe by the

Soviet Union. The countries that had previously been conceived as a *cordon sanitaire*, as a buffer zone *against* the Soviet Union, were now turned around, as it were, to serve as a buffer zone *for* the Soviet Union against the West. Although that had little to do with the principles of the Atlantic Charter that Roosevelt and Churchill had announced in August 1941, the USSR was to become one of the exclusive group making up the United Nations' Security Council with the right to veto its decisions. So, a country that had been expelled from the League of Nations on 14 December 1939 for its invasion of Finland would now play a decisive role on the global political stage.

The illusion of an amicable global government would not last long. It was not just that the Alliance was a collision of differing systems, philosophies, and divergent aims. The reason that their mutual alienation became almost complete by the end of the war was that Stalin thought of the world as a jungle. How could someone who did not trust even his closest advisers manage to trust a Roosevelt, a Churchill, or a Truman? That became ever clearer at the moment at which the common enemy was vanquished. At the Potsdam Conference, where the Big Three met between 17 July and 2 August 1945, it could have been predicted that the Alliance's days were numbered. Even the list of attendees was problematic. Roosevelt had died on 12 April and been replaced by his vice-president, Harry S. Truman, who was yet to build a reputation in international politics. Even less satisfactory was that, three days after the general elections on 26 July—that is, during the ongoing conference—Churchill was replaced by the new British prime minister, Clement Attlee. As a famous piece of documentary footage shows, Stalin did not even shake his proffered hand. Nevertheless, the conference was able to reach some conclusions.

There was broad agreement about the future of the German Reich, which was summed up in five key principles, the 'five Ds': denazification, demilitarization, democratization, decentralization, and deindustrialization. What was to happen with the rest of the world, on the other hand, was left open.

Not long beforehand, on 26 June 1945, no fewer than fifty countries had signed the Charter of the United Nations in San Francisco. But something that took place on the periphery of the conference at Potsdam was to prove far more momentous in the development of world politics. As though in passing, with conscious understatement, Truman mentioned to Stalin that the USA now had at its disposal a weapon with a hitherto unimagined power of destruction. Stalin seemed uninterested, according to those who witnessed it. But soon afterwards, the project of a consensual world government gave way to the division of the globe into two mutually hostile hemispheres, each of which armed for the bitter destruction of the other and whose areas of influence met and fought along a line drawn down the centre of Europe.

The mobilization of Soviet society

It was not only Soviet foreign policy that changed its stripes; changed, too, was the country in whose name it acted. For a short moment in the summer of 1941, it had not seemed certain that it would withstand the German onslaught and resist collapse. However, the German politics of occupation, as imprudent as it was bloody, would soon restabilize the Soviet state and the society at its base. The war made the Soviet people and their rulers partners in a common fate and simplified their divergent interests to a single aim: the fight for survival.

The common menace initiated a new, never-to-return social cohesion, a closeness between society, the Party, and the government, between rulers and ruled, that had never been known before. The only exception was the dictator himself, whose power had neither ever really been up for discussion nor ever would be. As before, he made all essential decisions alone, unapproachable and aloof from his countrymen, while the circle of lower-ranking advisers who tried to anticipate his wishes in the State Defence Committee remained small, limited, and easy to control. The war allowed Stalin to become ever more powerful. The collective experience of all crises having been overcome, all sacrifices and losses having at last been transformed into an overwhelming victory, all this ultimately elevated him into an almost mythic propaganda figure. His precise contribution to the victory and his countless political and military blunders could hardly be made out from the enormous distance at which his subordinates stood. So he became the definitive embodiment of victory, the 'Generalissimus' himself, in the official title with which he styled himself after 1945. The fact that this myth is still partly believed in Russia today gives an indication of the efficacy that it had then.

Nor was Stalin the only one to profit from the glamour of victory. It applied equally to his executive, above all to the Army and the Party. Despite all losses, the Communist Party was able greatly to increase its membership between 1941 and 1946, from 2.5 million to 4.1 million, having reached its nadir in winter 1941–2, when it had had only 1.1 million members. Even more striking was the eruptive growth of the Soviet Armed Forces, but more important even than these quantitative transformations were the self-confidence, respect, and influence that these two organizations gained in the national struggle with which they were so fundamentally identified. This, in turn, became the justification for the social privileges and powers that would continue to exist for the Army and the Party until 1989–90. It went without saying that all this could occur only under the overarching protection of the regent, that it was predicated on an individual and unconditional loyalty to Stalin.

At the same time, the war—as so often—proved to be an immense spur to modernization. The great wheels that the Soviet leadership had set in motion at the end of the 1920s—industrialization, urbanization, bureaucratization, and the increasing inclusion of women in the workforce—were all accelerated by the war's dynamism and by its requirements, regardless of whether they were real or putative. With the battle cry 'Everything for the front, everything for victory!', all economic efforts were now diverted into the armaments industry. Those who benefited—if such a term can be applied to the conditions of the time—were the industrial workers rather than the kolkhoz farmers, who remained the awkward stepchildren of this social transformation. The proportion of *kolkhozniki* in Soviet society continued its pre-war decline. Although those living in the countryside tended to be somewhat better off in food terms than those in the cities, even if officially there was no private property any more, they nevertheless had their own problems to contend with. Most of the Red Army's soldiers were conscripted from the countryside, and on top of this its last reserves had been extorted from it in a time of famine. Nor would those reserves be enough. Even before 1941, most Soviet citizens' standard of living had been lamentable, but now the rations were barely enough to exist on. 'Some workers are in such bad shape', it says in an official report from 1945, 'that they can't afford to be seen in public.' Without permanent improvisation, without a black market and such private means of production as the famous 'victory gardens', the ordinary Soviet citizen would hardly have made it through the war.

Since the men were often missing from home, the women had to replace them. The proportion of women among workers and employees had already been high in 1940, at 38 per cent, and by 1945 it had risen to almost 60 per cent. A similar ratio was eventually also reached in the agricultural sector. On the home front, women were everywhere: they directed traffic, worked in hospitals, offices, canteens, or railway stations, but also on production lines, wharfs, and even construction sites. Even the hardest physical labour was entrusted to them. Indeed, few of the stereotypes in official historiography ring so true as the hymns to the heroic women of the Great Patriotic War.

Another process that had been initiated long before 1941 and that now accelerated almost beyond recognition was the opening of the Soviet East. Under the direction of a specially instituted Evacuation Committee, it proved possible by January 1942 to transport between 1,700 and 2,000 industrial plants, 1,500 of considerable size, out of the grasp of the German conquerors. Raw material, means of transport, and even people were moved thousands of kilometres eastwards by train. Here, too, the efforts conformed to the familiar pattern: everything was thrown into motion, much was lost or destroyed on the way, but, in the end, an enormous relocation had in fact taken place. The beneficiaries were the area around the Urals as well as western and southern Siberia, in particular; in 1942–3, almost 40 per cent of Soviet capital was invested there.

In other sectors, too, the Stalinist regime succeeded in using all available means to mobilize absolutely everything that the country and people had to offer in service of the war. Even in the 1930s, the Soviet economy had been organized on a war footing; society's commitment and its capacity for suffering had already been subjected to an acid test, and people had already got used to experiencing the constant tension of knowing they were expected to surpass their capabilities. The war now provided ample opportunities for doing so. Defeating the 'fascist invaders', which, for the home front, meant working eight, ten, or twelve hours, seven days a week, did require iron discipline. But even more than that it necessitated a great rallying cry that all could understand. Neither Bolshevik ideology nor the threat of impending destruction could provide that, and a positive complement was needed. As a result, the war forced the Soviet Union, in a sense, to reinvent itself. What came out of it was Soviet patriotism, a very special amalgam of Soviet statehood with imperialist Russian colouring, of technical modernity and historical myth, mixed with individual relics of Bolshevik ideology. This paradigm shift struck a chord with Soviet society. Its deeply rooted patriotism, its long-hidden desire for national identity, now again and at last had something on which to project itself. It was as if the Soviet leadership had stumbled upon a magic word: the Great Patriotic War. It provided an almost messianic atmosphere of awakening passion, a *levée en masse*.

It would, of course, be wrong to suggest that the political and ethnic tensions in the Soviet 'family of peoples' were somehow dissolved, but they were temporarily concealed. At the same time, however, the regime had to demand enormous exertions from those peoples, exertions that were often beyond what they were able to give. Stalin possessed enough psychological sensitivity to recognize that propaganda alone, the ideological reduction of the cosmos to the Soviet fatherland, would not be sufficient.

This society could be totally mobilized only by taking the risk of loosening certain political, ideological, and economic controls. In the hour of need, it was not doctrine that had the highest priority, but rather pragmatism, individual initiative, and imagination.

Paradoxically, the war also brought freedom—not much freedom, but at least a taste. The media, universities, and above all the arts were the most reliable seismographs of this; Dmitri Shostakovich, for example, wrote about the ambivalence of living this kind of life:

> The war brought indescribable suffering and misery. Life became tough, very tough. There were endless grief, endless tears. But before the war it was even tougher, because everyone was alone with his suffering. Even before the war, there surely cannot have been a single family in Leningrad without losses...Then came the war. The secret, isolated grief became a common grief. You were allowed to speak about it, you could cry openly, openly weep for the dead. People no longer had to be afraid of their tears.

There was still a war, but was there not now also a thoroughly justified hope that, once it was over, Soviet society would be able publicly to discuss more than just grief? Constantine Simonov, an experienced correspondent from the front, wrote that 'life after the war seemed a celebration for which only one thing was needed—the final shot'.

The other side of the coin: Soviet war crimes and atrocities 1939–1945

In reality, however, the core of Stalin's system had remained the same. When locked into a battle for life and death, the regime was forced by circumstance to make some concessions to those it sent to fight that battle. But that cannot conceal the fact that, during the war, there was also a current running in the opposite direction. In the moment in which its existence was truly at stake, it was to be expected that the Stalinist dictatorship would defend itself even more brutally than it had when the threat had often been no more than a figment of its imagination. Seen from this perspective, the repression of the Soviet populace in those years was part of a continuing inner-Soviet process, which was also intimately connected with the course of the war.

At its outbreak, Soviet society still found itself in a state of shock; the experience of the years 1937–8, of the Great Terror, had struck deep. Moreover, the annexations of the years 1939–40 had triggered new 'mass operations'. At that point, around three million Soviet citizens were arrested and sentenced every year, almost 2 per cent of the population. Many ended up in the camp network of the Gulag, which had grown to include 425 work colonies by June 1941. In them, 1,930,000 prisoners scratched out an existence. There were another 200,000 in prison, awaiting sentencing or transport to the Gulag. Finally, 1,800 NKVD commandant offices governed 2,300,000 'special settlers'—that is, those unfortunates who had been deported into some godforsaken corner of the Soviet Union that they were then supposed to 'develop'.

'Every moment of life in the camp', wrote one of the prisoners, 'is a poisoned moment. There is much that a person is not allowed to know, not allowed to see, and if he has seen it—it's better that he die.' In 1938, 8 per cent of the prisoners did just that. During the war, it was even worse. Although 1.1 million prisoners were sent to the front, often in the *Shtrafbats*, the feared penal battalions, survival in the camps became even harder than before. In 1942–3 alone, 620,000 people succumbed to the merciless exploitation and the constant hardship. Incidentally, only a proportion of the prisoners were political. There were normal criminals, but the most numerous were people who had infringed one of the draconian new laws. Thus, during the war, more than 4.5 million people were sentenced for infringement of 'work discipline', theft of food, or other small misdemeanours, two-thirds of them to incarceration.

The Soviet system of repression was determined to keep these prisoners for itself. After the German invasion, around 750,000 were transported further east, sometimes under gruesome conditions. Where that was not possible, they were simply 'liquidated'. It is estimated that between 25,000 and 50,000 of them died in this way, most in prisons in the western Soviet Union. These Soviet crimes, which occurred in the initial phases of the war, made it easier for German perpetrators to disguise their own atrocities as retaliation. At the lower levels of the German Eastern Army, at least, that was wholeheartedly believed, perhaps because many of the war's foot soldiers recognized only vaguely what its leadership was really planning.

On top of this was the fact that the Red Army was initially harsh in the extreme in its treatment of prisoners of war. Of the between 170,000 and 200,000 German soldiers who fell into its hands between June 1941 and February 1943, 95 per cent did not survive their captivity; in fact, many did not even reach a prison camp. This changed only in 1943, *after* the Battle of Stalingrad, and then improved further in the years 1946–7. Nevertheless, Soviet captivity was deeply and rightly feared by the German soldiers. The number of German prisoners of war who went into Soviet captivity is calculated at between around 2.6 and 3.5 million; the proportion who died is estimated at 30 per cent, sometimes a little more, sometimes a little less. That is a significantly lower proportion than the proportion of Soviet prisoners who died in German hands (53 per cent), but still appallingly high.

The Stalinist Terror was directed not only at the enemy, but also at the Soviet 'family of peoples', mainly in the form of the arrests and deportations with which the Soviet leadership updated the system of exile implemented during Russia's Tsarist era. In order to ensure political conformity, individuals, communities, even whole ethnicities were 'disappeared' without the perpetrators' having to bother themselves with the legal, moral, or political dimensions of what they were doing. Four waves of deportation can be distinguished between the years 1939 and 1945. The first was in consequence of the annexations in the years 1939–40. Alone in what had been Eastern Poland, 320,000 people were forcibly relocated, around 100,000 were imprisoned, and thousands murdered. The fate of the 230,000 Polish soldiers was even more brutal; by the summer of 1941, only 82,000 of those in captivity were still alive. Among the victims were the almost 15,000 Polish officers whom the NKVD had murdered systematically. In April 1943, German troops discovered more than 4,400 corpses in mass graves at Katyn. Among the other 'brother peoples' that belonged to the USSR after 1939–40, 'anti-Soviet elements' were also arrested in droves: in Moldavia (26,000 people), in the new Ukrainian territories (around 89,000 people), and in the Baltic states (11,000 Estonians, 15,000 Latvians, and 18,000 Lithuanians).

The outbreak of war led to a second wave of deportations, which was made up now of Finns (50,000 people) and, above all, ethnic Germans. 'Get them out,' ordered Stalin in August 1941, 'so quickly that their feathers fly'. So the Autonomous Soviet Republic of Volga Germans disappeared. Of a total 1.4 million ethnic Germans, the majority were deported, estimates ranging between 700,000 and 1.2 million people. During the transport, mostly in cattle wagons or sometimes on foot, they died 'like flies', wrote one eyewitness, of hunger, thirst, or sometimes also suffocation in the packed wagons. The living conditions in their destinations in Siberia, Kazakhstan, or Uzbekistan were hard. In the first four years after deportation, the mortality rate among these special settlers was running at between 20 and 25 per cent.

The third wave of deportation broke in the year 1944. This time the victims of Stalin's politics of revenge were the Soviet Union's Muslim, often nomadic, peoples—Chechens and the Ingush (540,000 people), Karachays (85,000), Balkars (52,000), and Kalmyks (93,000), mainly peoples whom the Germans had allowed a relatively high level of autonomy during their short reign. In the second half of the year, the Caucasus and the Crimea were again purged of 'untrustworthy' nationalities; the victims were Crimean Tatars (191,000), Greeks, Bulgarians, Crimean Armenians, and Turks (37,000 but possibly also 58,000), as well as Meskhetian Turks, Kurds, and Hemshins (86,000 people).

The real hour of reckoning, however, came with the reconquest of the Soviet provinces first annexed in 1939–40, where there was a blanket accusation of having collaborated. The victims of this fourth wave of deportations, which continued essentially until 1953, were again the Finns (54,000 people), Estonians (31,000), Latvians (42,000), Lithuanians (236,000) western Ukrainians (153,000 people shot; 193,000 deported), and Moldavians (36,000). The numbers involved in this ethnic purge are horrifying. In fact, all of the USSR's non-Russian peoples were under *collective* suspicion of 'sabotage, spying and collaboration'. Sometimes that was

true, but it was more usual for people who had been totally unin-
volved to be classified as guilty. The persecutors were not in the
least interested in substantiating their generalized accusations, to
say nothing of striving for a degree of proportionality in their
response.

Nor is that the end of the story, one that is intimately bound up
with the Red Army, whose soldiers could feature as both victims
and executioners. They were subjected to a finely meshed surveillance conducted by SMERSH, the secret police specially constituted for that purpose, and it is estimated that every tenth Red
Army soldier acted as an informant. The penalties were severe.
'Cowards and traitors' were faced with either execution—during
the Battle of Stalingrad alone, 13,000 soldiers are estimated to have
lost their lives this way—or the penal battalions, into which a total
of 420,000 Red Army soldiers were drafted, or finally, the Gulag.
An idea of what it was like to live under such a system of constant
repression and terror is provided by this account from Alexander
Solzhenitsyn, who claimed—not without a certain irony—that
his imprisonment had probably been the easiest

> of all imaginable types. It didn't tear me from the embrace of my
> family, it didn't wrest me from the everyday domesticity that is so
> important to us. On a dull, tired, European day in February [1945],
> it grabbed me on one of the narrow spits of land on the Baltic,
> where we had surrounded the Germans or perhaps, it was unclear,
> they us—and tore me merely from my familiar troop section and
> from the impressions of the last three months of war.

The four hands of a pair of policemen grabbed 'simultaneously at
the star in my hat, my shoulder board, my belt, my map-case'.

But the Red Army's soldiers were not only victims; they often
functioned also as instruments of state (or sometimes wholly

private) terror. It was particularly bad during the advance onto German soil. 'You know very well that we've come to Germany to take our revenge,' wrote an artilleryman from his post in East Prussia. What this revenge consisted of can be guessed at from this report from Danzig: 'At the Trinitatis Cemetery, the mortuary was inhabited by people. The women were taken out between the graves and then shot in the pavilion, that was how the people who had hidden there were killed.' The Soviet occupation of the eastern German territories was far more than just a military operation. Until summer 1945, the orders of the day were tyranny, rape, and murder—'bad reactions' at the end of a 'chain of bad actions', as Golo Mann once put it. Nonetheless, one must be careful about generalizations here; officers such as Lev Kopelev or indeed Alexander Solzhenitsyn received heavy sentences after having been charged with 'compassion towards the enemy'.

Getting a quantitative grasp on these crimes and their consequences is no straightforward proposition. This is illustrated most simply by the significant variance between different calculations and estimates. There is evidence to suggest that a total of 13.2 million Germans either fled or were expelled from the eastern German territories as well as other parts of Central, Eastern, and South-Eastern Europe around 1944–5. The number of those who died in the process would then be put at 1,440,000. Three caveats need to be borne in mind: (1) These numbers are for refugees and expulsions from *all* areas of German settlement, in whatever country, that the Red Army occupied. (2) In this number are subsumed the victims of all atrocities and expulsions for which the local populations—Poles, Czechs, and so on—were responsible. (3) Finally, there is also debate over whether this estimate is not actually far too high, since it is derived from counts that are, in turn, based on 'unsolved cases' rather than on conclusively proven mortalities. As a result, there is also another set of calculations with considerably lower estimates: 600,000 or 500,000 or even 'only' between 75,000 and 125,000 victims. There is a similar range of variance in the estimates of the number of German civilians who were deported to become forced labourers in the Soviet Union. The figures range from 210,000 to 730,000 people, sometimes even 1,000,000, and the estimates of their mortality rate range between 20 per cent and 37 per cent.

Ultimately, nothing demonstrates the violence and absurdity of the Stalinist apparatus of repression as well as the fate of those who had suffered the most for the victory of the Soviet Union—the Soviet prisoners of war. The emaciated survivors of the German prison camps had been repatriated with high-flown rhetoric; as 'children of the fatherland', they were to be 'honourably welcomed home'. In truth, all were treated as suspicious. For example, one of them had to try to justify to his interrogator how it had been that he, 'as a Jew in the custody of the Germans, could have survived'. 'I said that no one had known I was a Jew...then he said to me: "that's what you all say", and hit me across the face.' In total, around 4.2 million Soviet citizens had to pay a terrible penalty for their time 'with the Germans', regardless of whether they were prisoners of war, forced labourers, or collaborators. Officers who had been taken prisoner and all members of the Vlasov Army were executed or sentenced to forced labour 'for ever'; ordinary soldiers were given shorter sentences or sent to the Far East, where they could expiate their guilt in the war against Japan. Most of those who had done forced labour for the Germans were treated comparatively leniently: the majority were let go, while the rest became forced labourers for a second time or were sent to the Gulag.

There is no question that the impulse here was ideology. But in these reactions it is also easy to see the psychological and moral abyss of a leadership that actually consisted of a relatively small number of people. As if their country had not already been sufficiently ruined by the enemy, they themselves drove it on into ever greater ruination. The Great Patriotic War wore many masks, but underneath all of its optimistic appearance, all the combat paintings, the army choirs, and colossal memorials, there remained the true and unchanging face of Stalin's tyranny.

8

War 1943–1945

1943: the turn of the tide

Stalingrad, the great battle that raged as 1942 became 1943, was a historical caesura, and for many contemporaries it was also a powerful symbol, but one thing it was not was a mortal blow to the German military. Even after the capitulation of the German Sixth Army (which was drawn out from 31 January to 2 February 1943), the war continued. This was because the Red Army substantially failed to exploit the crisis on the southern flank of the German front. In February 1943, there was suddenly a 300-kilometre-wide gap stretching across that front, and a Soviet advance to the Black Sea seemed likely, in the direction of Rostov. This 'super-Stalingrad' would have destroyed the German Army Group Don while simultaneously cutting off Army Group A, which was still fighting in the Caucasus. It was only a counter-attack led by Field Marshal Erich von Manstein, who took the strategic risk of allowing the Soviets to advance beyond their lines of supply before engaging them, that prevented a complete collapse of the southern section of the front. In truth, it was a military

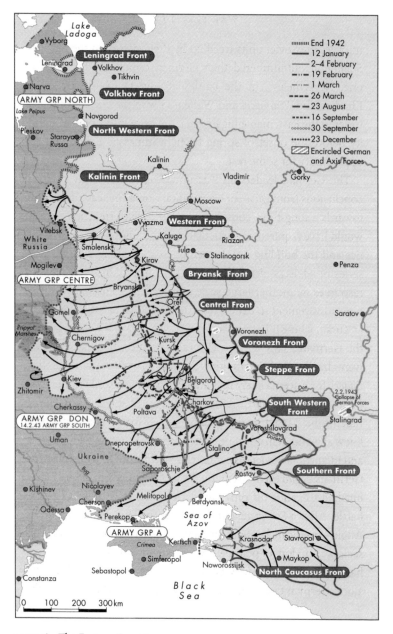

MAP 6. The Eastern Front in 1943

miracle; the Soviet units freed up by their victory in the Battle of Stalingrad outnumbered their German opponents by seven to one. Nevertheless, in the battles around Dnipropetrovsk and Kharkov, the *Wehrmacht* and Waffen-SS won the last German victories in the East, managing to patch the front into a kind of stability before the onset of spring brought impassable mud and the opportunity for some rest.

The German leadership was unwilling to draw any political conclusions from this—or even military ones. Instead of working towards a long-term consolidation of the Eastern Front—which would have required, in particular, a shift to mobile, defensive tactics and the building-up of reserves—Hitler, along with a whole series of advisers, decided literally to pulverize his own military resources in another large-scale offensive. The idea was to use a pincer movement to cut off the outward bulge of the Soviet front at Kursk, where it had expanded westwards into the join between the German Army Groups Centre and South. But the problems were already starting to multiply during preparations for Operation *Citadel*, for it seems likely that politics and propaganda rather than military rationale were again the guiding principles. Again, far too much time passed in the planning, and, worse, the Soviet side knew all about it in advance. 'Every valley is bursting with artillery and infantry,' a Soviet officer noted in his diary. On 5 July 1943, the Germans began their assault on the well-fortified Soviet positions, but had to call it off only eight days later, at the climax of the battle. After a Soviet relief offensive in the Donets Basin and the Anglo-American landings in Sicily, a German offensive on this scale was no longer possible. What remained was something that has gone into the history books as 'the largest ever tank battle': 2,900 German tanks fought 5,000 Soviet ones. 'The air roars, the earth shakes, you think your heart is going to shatter in your chest and tear you open,' was how one Red Army soldier described the experience. Kursk was a battle of numbers, one that in its dimensions and strategies was reminiscent of the First World War, the difference being that it was fought with Second World War technology. The losses were accordingly high. In the eight days of their offensive, the Germans lost 57,000 men, of whom 15,000 were killed, and their opponents lost 70,000 men killed, missing, or taken prisoner. The losses during the operations connected to the battle around Kursk were higher still. By the end of August, 170,000 Germans had been killed, wounded, or gone missing in action, and the equivalent losses on the Soviet side are also estimated in the hundreds of thousands.

With that the German leadership had again thrown away everything that it had managed to gather for that year: reserves, material, the new heavy panzers, time, and—what will have been most sorely missed—the initiative. The tank battle ended not with the German conquest of Kursk, but with the liberation of Kharkov and Orel by the Red Army. After that, the southern and to a certain extent also the central section of the German front could no longer be held. In the second half of 1943, the Red Army was able to push the *Wehrmacht* step by step back towards the West; daily retreats of between 10 and 20 kilometres were no rarity. But at that point the Soviet armies still did not manage really to engage and destroy their opponents. What they gained in lieu were ever greater swathes of territory, including such cities as Kiev and Smolensk, as well as a number of bridgeheads on the western bank of the Dnieper, which the *Wehrmacht* had actually been supposed to use as a defensible natural barrier. In other words, by the end of 1943, the Red Army had not managed to drive the German occupiers out of the

Soviet Union entirely, but there could no longer be any doubt that precisely that was about to occur. It was now only a question of when and of what would happen afterwards.

1944: the collapse of the Eastern Front

Soviet propaganda afterwards referred to 1944 as the 'year of ten victories'. This a somewhat contrived claim—and it has been repeatedly criticized ever since, quite rightly. Reference to one Soviet victory in particular should, in any case, have been enough. Operation *Bagration* began on 22 June 1944. In a few short days, this onslaught of more than 2.5 million Soviet troops, supported by more than 45,000 mortars and heavy guns, 6,000 tanks, and 8,000 aeroplanes, destroyed the entire German Army Group Centre. Consisting of 500,000 men with 3,200 heavy guns, 670 tanks, and 600 aeroplanes, its position had been hopeless from the start. 'Our troops storm forwards like a mighty torrent that bursts over all barriers, sweeps away all obstacles and washes a wide area clean of dirt and muck,' wrote a Soviet war correspondent. For the other side, it was one single inferno. A German artillery officer reported that the impacts of the Soviet shells and bombs had come so close together that explosions, smoke, and fountains of earth had prevented them from seeing anything at all. Operation *Bagration* became by some distance the heaviest of all German defeats, a defeat involving such comprehensive losses that the memory of it was long overshadowed by that of the Battle of Stalingrad, for the simple reason that there were so few left on the German side to describe the destruction that *Bagration* had wrought. Although thousands of isolated German troops managed, after personal odysseys sometimes lasting several weeks, to fight their way back

ILLUSTRATION 7. Marching West: Soviet cavalry pass by the graves of German soldiers

to their own lines, the ranks of eyewitnesses were extremely thin, at least in Germany. The Army Group Centre had lost 400,000 men dead or captured—that is, 32 of its 40 divisions.

The opportunities that now presented themselves to the victorious, vastly superior Soviet armies were correspondingly extensive. Advancing right into the heart of the German Reich and ending the war in 1944 seemed thoroughly realistic. The Soviet leadership, however, was half-hearted in capitalizing on the situation. The Red Army instead halted on the borders of East Prussia and on the eastern bank of the River Vistula, in the suburbs of Warsaw. The Soviet soldiers in Poland watched, their guns lying idle, while the Polish Home Army's improvised uprising was miserably crushed. In August and September 1944, the Soviet advance on the borders of the Reich came to a complete stop. There are a number of reasons why this happened. In the case of Warsaw, the motives for not engaging the Germans were transparently political. The losses and efforts of the previous months were also an important factor, as were the overextended lines of supply and communication and also the way that discipline had sharply deteriorated among the units that had already marched onto German soil. However, another consideration weighed far more heavily than these: the Soviet military commanders were still extremely wary of their German opponents. That they were not invincible had long been established, but the Soviets had experienced again and again in the previous winters that the *Wehrmacht* had an astonishing capacity for regeneration. At that point, in summer 1944, that capacity had finally been exhausted. Nonetheless, the idea of the Germans' almost uncanny military abilities, the '*Wehrmacht* Myth', was to exert its influence one last time. That was why the Soviet leadership lacked the courage and decisiveness to take advantage of this unprecedentedly opportune position and strike Nazi Germany a final, fatal blow by seizing the Reich's almost undefended capital city. This trepidation should not diminish the significance of the victories that the Red Army did win in 1944. That was the year in which German occupation ended throughout the Soviet Union, something achieved largely through Operation *Bagration*.

The course of the war ran parallel in the northern and southern sections of the German–Soviet front. Between 14 and 27 January, 1.2 million Soviet soldiers broke through the German blockade to the east of Leningrad. In that moment, the isolated metropolis's slow martyrdom came to an end after 880 days of encirclement, by some distance the longest siege that a modern city has had to withstand. On the evening of 27 January, 324 guns fired a salute over the Neva. In the following weeks, the German front was pushed back to the area east of Estonia and Latvia. These were areas where the Red Army was no long arriving simply as liberator. By the end of the year, the Soviets had reoccupied the Baltic states with the exception of the western part of Latvia, where the remaining German forces, still 500,000 men, were to hole up as Army Group Kurland until the end of the war.

The Soviet troops gained even more ground in the south. By as early as spring 1944, they had managed to push the collapsing German units in the Ukraine back for more than 300 kilometres. The German troops were repeatedly encircled and, if they were not completely destroyed, often used the last of their strength to break out again towards the West. The events in the Crimea took on an even more dramatic aspect. The peninsula had become a trap for its German occupiers after Hitler had obstinately refused to withdraw them in time. The Soviet assault that began on 8 April could not be resisted for long. Of the 230,000 German and Romanian soldiers, 60,000 died

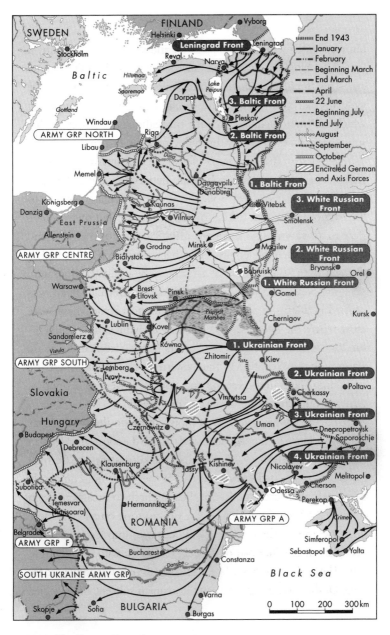

MAP 7. The Eastern Front in 1944

there while the other 150,000 were rescued in boats, under what were generally apocalyptic conditions. This is just another example of the catastrophic consequences for the German military of Hitler's insistence on having operational command. After that, the Red Army could not be stopped in the south either. Soviet troops mounted a major assault on 20 August against Army Group Southern Ukraine and thereafter occupied a number of territories in quick succession, first Romania, then the eastern part of Hungary, and, by the middle of October, also Bulgaria, which had, of course, not actually been at war with the Soviet Union. The Balkans started to become Soviet.

Hitler's almost hallucinatory fixations were not in the least affected by these developments. Untouched by this cascade of defeats, he informed his officers in December 1944 that the enemy could 'never count on capitulation, never, never'. How many Germans at that point were still following him out of conviction, how many out of habit, out of coercion, or out of fear of the 'Bolshevik hordes', is hard to estimate. What is certain is that the mentality of the German populace began to change fundamentally in the light of the momentous events being reported by the military. Also certain is that the increasing domestic brutality of the Nazi regime prevented this shift in mentality from being communicated to the outside world. In the end, only one course of action seemed open to either side: carrying on as before.

1945: the Soviet victory

The German–Soviet war did not run out of momentum, its armies did not tire of the struggle, and it was not decided, as in the final phase of a game of chess, by a few brilliant moves. Instead, the intensity of this ruinous, brutal, and merciless fight for existence stayed constant throughout its final days, and hundreds of thousands continued to go to their deaths. Only when there was literally nothing left to fight over, when almost all of Germany, right down to the Command Headquarters, had been occupied and Hitler himself had finally abdicated responsibility by means of suicide (30 April 1945), only then did the shooting stop.

The Red Army initiated this final act between 12 and 14 January by mounting an unstoppable offensive along the great curve of the Vistula. Their numerical superiority was again overwhelming, not least because Hitler had thrown the last German reserves—even at this late stage still numbering seven Armoured and fourteen Infantry Divisions—into action on the *Western* Front, where they staged a strategically pointless and militarily futile operation in the Ardennes (16 December 1944 to 21 January 1945). The Soviet side could not be seriously resisted; in only two weeks, the entire mass of soldiers, equipment, and weapons was able to advance another 300 kilometres west. 'The whole frontline is a sea of flames' was the impression of one Soviet artillerist. By the start of February 1945, the Soviet front was pushing into the Reich like an enormous spearhead; in central Germany, it was already at the Oder, fewer than a hundred kilometres from Berlin itself. But the attackers, too, had now temporarily expended much of their force, and there was a lull while they had gathered themselves for the final assault. Moreover, the battles raging to the sides of this giant spearhead had not yet burnt out—in Pomerania, they continued into March, in East Prussia and Silesia even into April. Another military crux point had formed on the Hungarian plains. Here, too, the Red Army was victorious. Budapest, which had fortified itself and defied the attackers for two months, fell on 11 February, followed on the 13 April by Vienna.

The war eventually ended in the place where it had been planned, in Berlin. Hitler was able to bring his idea of collective suicide to its conclusion with a 'final battle' for the Reich's capital. His influence on military decisions was evident to the last. He set himself up for a last stand in Berlin, the centre of the Reich, a metropolis in which almost three million people were still living, around two million of them women. The Soviet storm broke on 16 April 1945. Again there was very bitter fighting, especially on the Seelow Heights, where the German defenders initially managed to bring the Soviet shock troops to a standstill. But that was merely a short delay. A week later, Berlin was encircled. What followed was a disaster, a renewed orgy of killing that extended for another fortnight. 'Berlin is burning, there are only ruins left, there are weeping men and women walking on the roads to the East. So what, let them weep, after all they've had four years to laugh in,' wrote a Soviet artillery officer. In the smashed houses, ruins, and cellars of the dying city, the fighting ended only when the soldiers of the Red Army had fought their way into the centre of power and then down into the subterranean bunkers of the Reich Chancellery. After the signing of the German capitulation in the night between 8 and 9 May—in an officers' casino in the former school for sappers in Berlin Karlshorst—the guns finally fell silent.

The German's Reich's attempt, as reckless as it had been criminal, to subjugate the European continent and become a global power had ended in its own total ruin. Germany was occupied, the Nazi state demolished, Europe laid waste. The storming of Berlin alone had cost the lives of another 350,000 Soviet soldiers, 100,000 German soldiers, and an estimated 150,000 civilians. The centre of the Reich's capital city was 70 per cent destroyed;

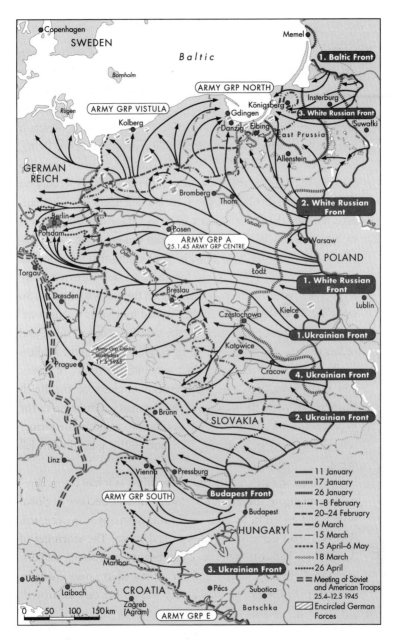

MAP 8. The Eastern Front in 1945

ILLUSTRATION 8. 'Victory!' Red Army soldiers on the roof of the Reichstag in Berlin at the end of April 1945

eyewitnesses described kilometre-long stretches of smoking rubble in which nothing had been left habitable. Nor was it by any means the only German city that the war reduced to this condition. All that was left of Hitler, who had first conceived Operation *Barbarossa* and then driven it onwards like no one else, were a few charcoaled bits of corpse, heaped together and thrown into a shell crater outside the bullet-riddled Reich Chancellery.

A military reckoning

Why did the German Reich lose this war? Why did the Soviet Union, in the archaic but precisely accurate formulation of one German general, become 'an agent of fate' for the *Wehrmacht*? Historians can make it easy for themselves and point to the overwhelming superiority in men and resources at the disposal of the vast Soviet empire. But the reality of war is far more than a simple matter of arithmetic and statistics. In the first weeks of the war in the East, there were moments when it was not at all certain which way the scales would tip. That applies particularly to the period of June and July 1941, which Andreas Hillgruber has rightly described as the 'zenith of the Second World War'. At that point, the Japanese High Command was seriously considering whether to catch the Soviet Union with a second pincer from the East. On 2 July 1941, the Japanese leaders decided to concentrate on the South-East Asian theatre instead. Whether the Soviet Union could have resisted a Japanese assault at that moment is highly doubtful.

Moreover, the *Wehrmacht* had already proved more than once how quickly it could deal with numerically superior opponents, even in difficult conditions. For instance, in the Balkan campaign, which many military officials at the time had considered a sort of dress rehearsal for *Barbarossa*, it was the precise combination of military professionalism and technological modernity, of speed, ideological dynamism, and totalitarian rigour that made the German Army so successful and so dangerous. Why, then, did it founder in the Soviet Union? Was it really only the weather—that they invaded too late in the year—or even just that the distances involved were on such a different scale?

In a military analysis, the obvious place to begin is at the top, with the High Command. As Commanders-in-Chief, both Hitler and, to an even greater extent, Stalin were complete amateurs. That did not prevent either from trying his hand as field marshal. Sometimes they made the right decisions, sometimes of course they had no option but to make the decision they did, but on other occasions they came to conclusions that—without taking the ideological dimension into account—could not have been more wrong, the most glaring example being the senseless and costly doctrine of holding military positions at any price. 'Is this common lack of wit and inspiration any wonder?', reflected Hellmuth Stieff (a major and later one of the 20 July conspirators, in January 1942), in the light of this style of command. Put simply, these two commanders-in-chief could do whatever they wanted, even when it came to the sensitive business of military management. In this, there was one telling difference between the two sides, in that the Soviet Union's resources meant that it could allow itself many more command errors than the German Reich.

It is also striking how poorly the German side had prepared for Operation *Barbarossa*. Everything was lacking: knowledge of the enemy, provisions, the correct weapons and equipment, stocks of fuel, ammunition, and spare parts and, above all, proper planning of the operation itself. This was not the fault solely of the upper echelons of the German military. Their fault was, rather, that they offered too little resistance to Hitler's demands and that they placed their hope in 'military logic' reasserting itself once things were underway. This was particularly evident in the overall strategy of the German campaign. The frontal offensive by three Army Groups was nothing better than a compromise between the notions put forward by Hitler, whose aims were primarily economic or ideological, and those of the German military leadership. To them it was clear that in this case, as in all others, Clausewitz's famous maxims must apply: an offensive operation can never be too strong, and it must be directed at a single, decisive point. No single point seemed to present itself quite so well as Moscow, the heart and brain of the Soviet empire. Instead, however, of concentrating the numerically inferior German offensive forces on this (or at least on some other) single goal, the Army Groups were pulled wide apart and distributed along a broad front. 'A strategy without a focal point is like a man without a character,' General Field Marshal Paul von Hindenburg once wrote. He knew what he was talking about.

There is another striking difference between the German and Soviet leaderships. While the Soviet Armed Forces were kept under almost prison-like control by the Stalinist apparatus, they gained an increasing freedom of action during the course of the war, albeit within the parameters of Stalin's dictatorship. The reverse happened to their German opponents, who were subjected ever more closely to Hitler's mania of control. Ultimately, it made its presence felt at every level of the Army. 'There are actually only two possibilities,' wrote a German soldier towards the end of the war, 'death from an enemy bullet or from the henchmen of the SS'. That description is very similar to the conditions in which the Red Army had been living in 1941. This keeping on a short leash would also have a deleterious effect on the operational level. Naturally, it would be completely wrong to follow the many generals who after 1945 attributed all responsibility for failures of leadership to Hitler individually, for completely obvious motives. But it is undeniable that many of the military catastrophes in the second half of the war bear the fingerprints of the *Führer*. What was more serious, however, was that, after winter 1941–2, he was no longer able, nor in fact even willing, to develop so much as the rough outline of a convincing strategic and operational approach.

Let us now widen our view to take in the German and Soviet commanders on the ground. Any comparison quickly shows the excellence of the German professional soldiers in tactical leadership. It was no accident that four Soviet soldiers were killed for every one German. After the Purges in the Red Army, the officer corps initially contained little in the way of military competence. Only 10 per cent had been in the Army long enough to be able to draw on the experience of the First World War. The new officers, who had been promoted into positions of command after the Purges, were at first completely out of their depth. But they learned: they had no choice but to learn in an effort to catch up with their opponents.

There were, however, branches of the *Wehrmacht* that were criminally neglected, first among them military intelligence and logistics. For many of the German military, the Soviet Union remained no more than an unknown vastness whose capabilities were alternately over- and underestimated. One of the main figures in the German resistance, the well-informed Ulrich von Hassell, wrote on 15 June 1941 that the military assessed the prospects for a 'rapid victory over the Soviets' as 'reassuringly favourable'. The supply of the million-strong German Army was equally unprofessionally handled, as was starkly demonstrated, if it had not already been before, during the first winter of the Soviet campaign. 'That it gets cold in Russia at this time of year'—as one officer on the German General Staff wrote sarcastically—'should actually be the ABC of an Eastern campaign.' These were not the only shortcomings of the German High Command; suffice it to mention the military and psychological errors made in the war against the partisans or in the politics of their occupation. Naturally, the central policies came directly from the *Führer* HQ, but too many military leaders accepted them or even thought along similar lines, despite there being groups within the *Wehrmacht* who wanted to bring the local populations on side by granting limited concessions. The inability of these reformers to assert themselves was not simply a consequence of the totalitarian nature of the Nazi regime nor one of the internal dynamics of the war against the partisans. Its roots also lay in the self-conception of an army that had little experience of administering occupied areas and colonies, or of dealing with indigenous uprisings.

A technological comparison is also very telling. Although both armies found themselves in the middle of a radical shift during the war, the Red Army was significantly quicker off the mark. What is more, the Soviets also succeeded in modernizing both qualitatively *and* quantitatively. While the German side may well have been superior to its opponents in the development of certain high-tech weapons systems, the production numbers of those weapons remained small. The Soviet Armed Forces had relatively few types of modern, effective weapons available to them, but those they did have, they had in masses. This situation was precisely reversed for their German opponents: an endless array of types, but no strength in depth.

This was compounded by the Soviet advantage of having lines of supply that were 'internal' and hence comparatively short. Not only were the Germans' supply lines far longer; they also failed to build up an adequate transport system in the occupied Soviet territories. Supply by means of lorries broke down as early as the first months of the war and was subsequently possible only over short distances, while the railway network was limited to a small number of trunk lines that were very vulnerable to disruption. Even more amateurish, to say nothing of the moral implications, was the German High Command's idea that the troops would simply take all they needed from the country they were passing through. In the final analysis, Operation *Barbarossa* lacked a solid material and logistical basis right from the beginning, and here, too, it was ideology that was supposed to make up the shortfall.

Ironically enough, ideology did ultimately tip the balance, but in a quite different way from the one expected by the German planners. Long before, Clausewitz and Caesar knew that there are three things one needs to master in winning a war: the enemy's armed forces, his territory, and, lastly, his people's will to resist. The armed forces had to be destroyed and the country occupied, but it was only when the opponent's will to resist had been broken or won over that the war would truly be at an end. The German leadership, by contrast, were so foolhardy that they waged war from the beginning, not only against the Soviet Union with its superior resources, but also against almost all of its peoples at the same time. Hitler and his entourage did not think it necessary to make even tactical allowances for the scale of the task, and steadfastly ignored the enormous political opportunities that presented themselves, especially in summer 1941, when the *Wehrmacht* was often being joyfully received in the Soviet Union's westernmost territories and desertion was threatening to undermine the very existence of the Red Army. The German leaders, however, were determined not to make any alteration to their idea of how the war would be conducted, which meant destruction, exploitation, and oppression. Only once it was already too late, in autumn 1944, were they prepared to open the door—as with the Vlasov Army—to a certain political flexibility.

It is hardly surprising that their enemies' concept of a Great Patriotic War would prove far more powerful—not least because justifications of defence always seem more plausible than those of invasion. The German campaign of annihilation left little room for questions, interpretations, or alternatives, with the result that only a minority of Soviets ever collaborated with the Germans, in spite of the fact that so many in Soviet society might otherwise have been predisposed towards collaboration with the invaders for manifold political, ethnic, personal, or ideological reasons. Instead, they fought for their freedom, even if that was something of a relative term under Stalin's regime—or they fought simply to survive. The Great Patriotic War was far more than a propaganda construct; it became a political reality. It became the central concern of millions of Soviet citizens, and that alone made the foundering of the German strategy inevitable.

9

Aftermath

The endpoint: Europe in May 1945

By May 1945, the war had been won and lost. The map of Europe left no doubt about that. The first thing one noticed was the enormous hole that had opened up in the middle of the continent. The few positions and zones that the *Wehrmacht* still held were of little account; they existed only because the Allied offensives had decided to spare them. Germany was no longer one of the group of powers by whom Europe's future would be directed. After the unconditional capitulation of the German Wehrmacht on the 7–9 May in Reims and Berlin, and the arrest in Flensburg on 23 May of what remained of the Reich's executive, the 'Dönitz government', Germany's future was no longer in its own hands. It had become a counter in global politics. On 5 June, the four Allied Commanders-in-Chief in Berlin announced that they were now assuming the role of government. In the subsequent Potsdam Conference, the post-war order began to take shape.

What was striking about a bird's-eye view of Europe was not only that the continent had lost its political centre; it was now also very obviously divided. Europe had disintegrated into two fundamental blocs, three if one looked a little closer. The Eastern part had been occupied by the Red Army. In the previous months the Red Army had fought its way further West, very much further. In this way, Stalin not only definitively secured the territorial prizes of the years 1939–40; he also placed Soviet troops in Bulgaria, Romania, Hungary, Poland, Czechoslovakia, and, last by but no means least, the eastern part of the erstwhile Greater German Reich. On 25 April, Soviet and American troops shook hands in the Saxonian town of Torgau, on the river Elbe. From now on, two worlds would confront each other across a line drawn through Germany—'the East' and 'the West'.

On one side, there was the Western Allies' sphere of influence. To it belonged Western Europe as well as central and southern parts of the continent. The Western Allies' occupation of Italy could only really be described as an 'occupation' in the technical sense of the term, and even that ended rapidly, on 31 December 1945. Furthermore, a very large majority of the Italian public had welcomed the invading Allied troops as liberating them from the nightmare of the collapsing Fascist regime and the subsequent German occupation. That was even more distinctly the case in France and the Benelux states. Although there were those who lost out—as in any historical shift—the overwhelming celebrations with which the advancing Allied troops were greeted in 1944–5 left no room for doubt about how much most of the people living there had longed for an Allied victory. Despite all their losses, it initially seemed self-evident to France and especially Great Britain that they would again take up their mantles as great European and colonial powers. How difficult that would be and how comprehensively the war had drained both these countries would come to light only in the course of the following years. There was a special case in the Western Allies' sphere of influence—namely, Greece, where the British landing in October 1944 was soon followed by the outbreak of a bitter civil war between the conservative and communist forces, which ended only in 1949. In contrast, peace finally reigned throughout Western Europe as well as in Italy, Denmark, and Norway; and after the return of the governments-in-exile, political normality soon re-established itself in democratic and constitutional forms.

Peace reigned also in the eastern half of Europe. But this was a different kind of peace, and the Soviet Union soon began to transform the constellation of countries there on its own model into a series of satellite states. Whereas the USA, unsure about its continuing strategy and slowed down by all kinds of European and domestic American considerations, hesitated at first about whether and to what extent it wanted to engage in post-war Europe, the Sovietization of Eastern Europe was brought about unscrupulously and with unimaginable brutality. 'This war is not like those of the past,' Stalin told a confidant in April 1945. 'Whoever occupies a territory installs his own social system in it. Everyone introduces his own system as far as his armies can reach. That's the way it has to be.'

But by no means all of Europe's states belonged securely to one of the two power blocs. These anomalies came about in a number of different ways. Yugoslavia, Finland, and Albania—three potential candidates for inclusion in the Soviet power bloc—all managed to evade the Stalinist grasp. Some countries remained neutral: Switzerland, Austria (which had declared its independence on 27 April 1945), Sweden, Ireland, and initially also Turkey, although the political and historical reasons for their neutrality were very diverse. The final members of this group were Spain and Portugal, the two last relics of the authoritarian–fascist regimes of the inter-war period. The survival of these two dictatorships, which seemed rather anachronistic against the background of Europe's new political order, was possible only because they had kept themselves to a great extent out of the war.

The bottom line was that the divided continent could no longer act as if it were the centre of the world—a mere glance at the map was enough to demonstrate this. Such a situation brought benefits as well as disadvantages. On the one hand, Europe was no longer left to the mercy of its own isolationism, its inauspicious traditions and circular conflicts. That the exhausted and ruined continent would ever again drag the rest of the world into one of its spasms of self-annihilation, or indeed that it would ever regain its rank as an independent political power, then seemed almost inconceivable. On the other hand, Europe was now more or less dependent on the two superpowers. Soon enough, the Cold War and the terrible prospect of nuclear overkill would stretch like a long shadow across much of the world—and the mood was at its darkest in Europe. This was where the conflict's deepest fault lines ran, almost precisely where the Eastern hemisphere had collided with the Western at the conclusion of the Second World War. Trapped under the glacier of the cold war, it was a historical moment that remained preserved as if in ice. When a German journalist, moved by the events of 9 November 1989, said that *this* was the day on which the Second World War had finally come to an end, it served only to underline what far-reaching consequences this epochal conflict decades before had carried in its wake.

The outcome

When the war was over, life went on, not by any means for every-one but nevertheless—although it sometimes hardly seemed credible—for the majority. The number of those who did not sur-vive the war was not small, particularly not in the Soviet Union. Other than China, no country involved in the Second World War had to bear such heavy losses.

No one knows what the precise figures are. Everything that hap-pened was simply too large, too chaotic—and often impossible to document in the way we would have liked. Moreover, any totting-up of the dead faces significant methodological problems, as well as being hedged around with qualifications, arising from both political and psychological motives. The Soviet leadership was not interested in finding the exact number of victims, for obvious reasons. It was only with the politics of 'openness' (glasnost) that the archives were unlocked and light was let in on the subject. But in Germany, too, it took a long time for reliable statistics to become available. This was in part the expression of a telling lack of interest among the Germans, in part also of hope or of a refusal to accept what had occurred. People in Germany were more preoccupied in the period immedi-ately after 1945 by the widespread rumours about Soviet camps in which prisoners of war were prohibited from contacting the outside world. Thankfully, all that now belongs to the past. International research has reached a position from which it can at least set limits to the numbers of the dead. There is space here for those figures—but not for all, because a listing of the statistics for all the victims from all the states that were somehow affected by the Hitler–Stalin war would be far beyond the remit of this book. The losses of the two main antagonists would require a chapter in their own right.

It has been estimated that the Soviet Union lost a total of 26.6 million people in the Second World War. Of those, 11.4 million were members of the Soviet Armed Forces who died as a result of the fighting itself or in German captivity (around 3 million of the latter). All other victims were civilians, 15.2 million of them. A monstrous figure, reminding us once again just what kind of a war this was. Some groups among this mass of victims are widely familiar—for example, the 2.4 million Soviet Jews who lost their lives in the Holocaust; or the Leningraders who succumbed to the German siege and whose number is estimated at between 600,000 and one million; or the 500,000 people who were killed in the war with the partisans. The traces of the other civilian casualties, more than 11 million people, have often been submerged in the terrible fog and chaos of this gigantic war. We do have casualty statistics for individual cities, camps, periods, or even groups; for example, 1.3 million children were killed. But these specific tallies do not allow us to assign all of the casualties to this or that event and so find a structure within it. All that is known is that these people died on either one side or the other of the German–Soviet lines and sometimes in-between them. What we should take care to keep in mind while counting the victims, a task that is really just one long indictment, is that a part of the responsibility for them, albeit a smaller one, is borne by the Stalinist regime, and not only because it waged its half of the war without regard for the costs to its own people. As we have seen, its criminality was expressed in more than one sphere of action.

Compared with the Soviet equivalents, the number of German dead is not so high, although it should not be forgotten that on their side the demographic basis was quite different. Since the end of the 1990s, we have known that total German military losses were

ILLUSTRATION 9. Behind the scenes: a Soviet officer, a 'Hero of the Soviet Union', on the day of the great victory parade in Moscow, 26 June 1945

actually far higher than had long been believed: close to 5,318,000 men. Of those, around half, 2,743,000, fell on the Eastern Front.

It is far harder to get a handle on the number of German civilians whose lives were claimed by the war in the East. Suffice it to cite again the calculation that 1.4 million Germans found their deaths as a result of fleeing or being driven from their homes. To those would be added—according to this calculation—the

270,000 deaths among those who were deported for forced labour in the USSR and the further 310,000 dead among the ethnic Germans deported from within the USSR. As mentioned above, the size of these groups has also been estimated as far smaller.

Moreover, a proportion of those Germans who died as a result of the war from the air were killed by Soviet bombs and the total number of victims is estimated at between 380,000 and 635,000, the most likely figure seeming to be 465,000. As early as August 1941, Berlin was attacked by a small number of long-range Soviet bombers, but the Soviet threat from the air remained minimal until 1944. It built to a crescendo in 1945, which was—seen from an overall perspective—so late in the day that only a relatively small proportion of the Germans killed in bombing raids died as a result of Soviet attacks. Finally, we should not forget one last group of victims: at least 44,000 Germans died in the ten special camps that the Soviet military administration erected on its newly occupied territory in 1945.

These are all merely thin, neat lists of figures and we can only guess at the countless tragedies that stand behind them. Perhaps it would be easier to grasp if we reminded ourselves that this is the totting-up of something that could mean people shot, run over, burnt, slashed, mutilated, starved, frozen, hanged, and much else. Can statistics, which are often vague and provisional, but also abstract and sober, ever really do justice to such suffering? Human suffering cannot simply be added up like a balance sheet. Nonetheless, its dimensions become truly distinct only in figures. They alone give these events a common denominator.

In any case, the survivors had to continue to live with these losses, all of which were personal. It was not all they inherited from the war. It is usual for the number of the dead to be smaller than that of a war's other victims: invalids, the physically and psychologically wounded, widows, orphans, the destitute, the lost, and the homeless. Many of them struggled to find their feet again in civilian life. The way the war could change those who fought it was strikingly written about by one Soviet nurse:

> In war, one thing is as bad as the other... The pilots have it rough, the armoured corps and the artillerymen—everyone has it rough, but all of that is nothing compared with how it is for the infantry... Right after an attack, it's better not to look into their faces, there's nothing human in them, they've somehow become completely alien. I just can't describe how it is. You get the feeling you're surrounded by the mentally ill. It is a terrible sight.

A kind of sequel is provided by a German psychiatrist's report on his impressions of soldiers after the war. About one of his patients, a former captain, he wrote that he no longer thought of himself as a person, all he now felt was a blank. The battles were in the past and with them the excitement of battle. All that was left was a complete emptiness, a collective burn-out.

The human losses were echoed by the physical and material ones. By 1945, in the Soviet Union alone, 1,710 towns and around 70,000 villages had been razed to the ground. The total damage suffered by the Soviet Union is estimated—at 1941 prices—at 67.9 billion roubles, which corresponds to around 30 per cent of the country's fixed capital at the outbreak of war. If the direct expenditure on financing the war is included—55.1 billion roubles—along with the recession experienced by the Soviet economy, total Soviet losses come to around 184 billion roubles. Other appraisals have put this figure significantly higher.

Calculating how much the Second World War cost Germany is more difficult, particularly if one wants to isolate the costs of one front. Nevertheless, we know that the total expenditure of the German Reich between September 1939 and May 1945 ran to a total of 1,471 billion Reichsmark, to which occupied, allied, and neutral countries added 90.3 billion Reichsmark in the form of contributions and occupation costs. This total does not include the supplementary financial contributions by the private sector. To these must also be added the material losses, which were estimated at between 550 billion and 620 billion RM, plus 75 billion RM in property losses for those driven from their homes, as well as the costs of occupation until 1955 and 1958 (in the GDR), which came to 88.4 billion RM, and finally the losses incurred by currency reform in 1948, which were estimated at 56 billion RM. In short: the Germans had not been so thoroughly destitute since the end of the Thirty Years War.

But it was about more than just money or goods. A relatively short-term problem posed by the end of the war was what to do about the German prisoners of war. By summer 1947, their number had risen to 8.7 million, collapsing back down to 500,000 by January 1949. The Soviet Union refused for a long time to release a last contingent of more than 11,500 who had been found 'guilty' and who finally reached their homeland only in 1955–6. A more protracted set of problems was posed by the German refugees from the former eastern part of Germany and from Eastern Europe in general. The end of the German–Soviet War initiated a mass migration without parallel, flowing in the opposite direction to what those who started it had intended. After the forced deportations that the German authorities had carried out in the Soviet Union and above all in Eastern Europe, it was now the turn of the Germans living in the east of their country or of Europe to experience this suffering. With them disappeared a world that stretched

Wer kennt ihn?

Leutnant
Heinz Krüger
geb. 24.3.1919 in Eberswalde
Heimatanschrift
Breslau, Clausewitzstr. 4

Feldpost-Nr. 19812 A
Vermißt seit 14.1.1945
bei Radom, Polen

ILLUSTRATION 10. Missing: a German mother looking for her son at the refugee camp at Friedland, 1955, shortly after the return of the last German Prisoners of War from the Soviet Union back generations. Although the number who lost their lives to flight and exile has still not really been clarified to this day, we know how many people were left at the end. By 1950, 7.7 million refugees had reached West Germany, while another 4.1 million had arrived in the GDR.

Looking from a wider perspective, we can see that not only people, landscapes, traditions, and even nations had been destroyed. A whole world lay in ashes—that of both of the erstwhile opponents and, of course, all the countries that lay between them. The Soviet Union contributed a great deal to this terrible situation, but the actual initiative for all of it came from Germany, and not just once but on three distinct occasions: in 1939, when the German leadership unleashed a war in Europe; in 1941, when it spread the war to the rest of the world; and, finally, after the winter of 1942–3, when these sorcerers' apprentices of national socialist revolution proved too incompetent and too downright cowardly to admit to themselves that it had all been a mistake—even if only in its strategy, to say nothing of its ideology. What was left them then was the fascination of their own downfall. This—at the very latest—should have been the hour of the German resistance. But that hour never came.

In the end, the Soviet Union had won, it had become larger and more powerful—but at what cost? Its transition from war to peace turned out to be just as difficult. A shattered, weakened nation first had literally to find itself again. Millions of people were trying to find their homes or at least someone they knew. Their misery was indescribable, and neither the deliveries of goods from Germany nor the exploitation of German deportees and prisoners of war, which at the time accounted for up to 10 per cent of German GNP, could change that. There were shortages of everything—of food, consumer products, houses, infrastructure, energy, retraining and educational programmes, and medical care, as well as of an administration worthy of the name. On top of that came the end of the Anglo-American deliveries, the terrible drought of 1946 and the subsequent famine that claimed the lives of between 500,000 and 1,000,000 people, the comparatively high degree to which the Red Army stayed mobilized, sucking in resources, and, last but not least, the internal 'counter-offensive' to which the Stalinist regime switched after the end of the war. All the careful political corrections and concessions made during the war were soon reversed. In consequence, the gigantic twilight world of the Gulag began to grow anew. At the beginning of the year 1953, the Gulags contained a total of 2,450,000 prisoners as well as another 2,750,000 'special settlers'. This apparatus was, moreover, reaching the limits of its capacity: it became even more expensive and ineffectual, and even its administrators began to cause problems, so that, by the end, the cases of refusal to work, break-outs, or even revolts were becoming increasingly frequent. The real caesura, however, came only with the amnesty of 27 March 1953, barely three weeks after Stalin's death, which gave 1,200,000 prisoners their liberty.

But that is another story. In the years before it, the disillusionment of the Soviet people could hardly have been greater. 'In the war, life was hard,' wrote one woman from Moscow, 'but it wasn't humiliating, we expected something better, we hoped. But now life will be even harder and we have no hope that it will improve.' All that some people had left to hold on to was the memory of victory in the Great Patriotic War, that most bittersweet triumph, and at that time also—as strange as it may seem from a contemporary perspective—faith in Stalin. The way that the war is remembered, at least, has changed very little to this day.

The Germans emerging from Hitler's influence and the exhaustion of the war had memories of their own, lots of them, but hardly memories that would have served to motivate them. The upswing of the previous twelve years had ended in total ruin—militarily, politically, economically, and above all morally. It left behind a deeply wounded society in which everything seemed worthy of suspicion and which now, out of necessity, began to rebuild in the remnants of what had been the Greater German Reich. It had lost a quarter of its landmass, which was now 'administered' by Poland and the USSR; the rest was occupied by the four Allied powers. Each of those was now to govern the chaos in his own zone.

Joint government of the whole of Germany by an Allied Control Council soon proved to have been an illusion. Nor was there any more talk of plans to divide the country into several states, because a completely different type of division was already taking shape. And something else was rapidly becoming apparent: that a former great power in the centre of Europe required more than just a political programme aiming at cleansing, punishment and 're-education', reparations and weakening, and otherwise providing nothing except a few more or less scanty supplies. The victorious powers began to move towards taking the risk of a new beginning, a cautious move towards German autonomy, from 1947–8 onwards. It went well, partly because the war, even more so than in the Soviet Union, had laid the tracks for rapid post-war development. It was precisely the defeat and the loss—as bitter as that is—that became the basis of a far-reaching modernization, a renewal that left hardly any aspect of Germany or the Germans untouched. But that, too, is another story.

In 2011, seventy years after the launching of Operation *Barbarossa*, the youngest participants in that war have become old men and women. Personal, first-hand recollection of the war is becoming ever rarer; it will not be long before it has disappeared for good. That alone is a reason why this war of wars will come to seem ever more distant. We will miss those memories as we will miss those who keep them, not least since it was partly those memories that ensured even in the hottest phases of the cold war that there would not be another military conflict on such a scale.

Does that mean that the German–Soviet War has become merely a matter of historical curiosity, one of the innumerable struggles in the annals of world history, unreachably remote and abstract, similar to the Punic War or the Seven Years War? Hardly. As I said above, since 1945 there has been nothing in the Western hemisphere of a scale comparable to that of the Second World War. One pivot of that global conflict, indeed the moment of its greatest intensity, was the war between Nazi Germany and the Stalinist Soviet Union. For us to ignore or even forget that, the world would have to witness an event of comparable proportions. And may God forbid it.

CHRONOLOGY OF EVENTS

1939

23	Aug.	The Nazi–Soviet Non-Aggression Pact
1	Sept.	Germany invades Poland without declaring war. Beginning of the Second World War in Europe
3	Sept.	Great Britain and France declare war on Germany
17	Sept.	Beginning of the Soviet invasion of eastern Poland
28	Sept.	German–Soviet Boundary and Friendship Treaty

1940

11	Feb.	German–Soviet Economic Treaty
9	Apr.	German attack on Denmark and Norway
10	May	Germans begin their offensive in the West, violating the neutrality of the Netherlands, Belgium, and Luxembourg
22	June	Franco-German armistice
28	June	Beginning of the Soviet invasion of eastern Romania (Bessarabia and north Bukovina)
21	July	Incorporation of the Baltic states of Estonia, Latvia, and Lithuania into the USSR
31	July	The first major conference between Hitler and the leadership of the *Wehrmacht* to discuss the plan for an attack on the Soviet Union
27	Sept.	Tripartite Pact between Germany, Italy, and Japan
12–13	Nov.	Soviet Foreign Minister Molotov visits Berlin without agreement
18	Dec.	Hitler signs Directive No. 21 (Code Name Barbarossa). Preparation for the invasion of the Soviet Union begins

1941

30	Mar.	Hitler's speech to the chiefs of the *Wehrmacht*, urging that the war against the Soviet Union be waged with the utmost harshness
22	June	German invasion of the Soviet Union (Operation *Barbarossa*). The war between Germany and the USSR begins
22–27	June	Italy, Romania, Slovakia, Finland, and Hungary declare war on the USSR
2	July	The Japanese government decides against an attack on the Soviet Union
12	July	Anglo-Soviet Agreement on Mutual Assistance
5	Aug.	Conclusion of the Battle of Smolensk. Around 310,000 Soviet soldiers are taken prisoner
8	Sept.	Leningrad is largely surrounded by German troops
19–26	Sept.	German troops take Kiev, conclusion of the Battle of Kiev: around 665,000 Soviet soldiers are taken prisoner
28–30	Sept.	Germans massacre over 33,000 of Kiev's Jews in the Babi Yar ravine near the city
2	Oct.	The German attack on Moscow begins
20	Oct.	Conclusion of the Battle of Vyazm and Bryansk. Around 673,000 Soviet soldiers are taken prisoner
5–6	Dec.	Beginning of the Soviet counter-offensive before Moscow
7	Dec.	Japanese attack on the US Pacific Fleet at Pearl Harbor
8	Dec	USA declares war on Japan
11	Dec.	Germany and Italy declare war on the USA

1942

1	Jan.	The 'United Nations Pact': the signatories pledge that they will not make a separate peace with Germany, Italy, or Japan

20	Jan.	Wannsee Conference, Berlin: leading Nazis and ministerial officials meet to discuss the 'Final Solution of the Jewish Question'
7	June–1 July	German troops take Sevastopol in the Crimea
11	June	Mutual Aid Agreement between the USA and the USSR
28	June	The German summer offensive on the region to the east of Kursk and Kharkov begins
9	Aug.	Germans take the Maykop oilfields, which have already been destroyed
12–15	Aug.	Summit meeting between Stalin, Churchill, and Harriman in Moscow
23	Aug.	German troops break through to the river Volga, north of Stalingrad
7–8	Nov.	Allied landings in Morocco and Algeria
22	Nov.	The German Sixth Army (around 250,000 men) is surrounded in the Stalingrad region

1943

14–25	Jan.	Allied Casablanca Conference: at which the demand for the 'unconditional surrender' of Germany, Italy, and Japan is first formulated
31	Jan.–2 Feb.	Surrender of the German Sixth Army at Stalingrad
18	Feb.	Goebbels speaks at the Sportpalast in Berlin: 'Do you want total war?'
5–13	July	Failure of the German Operation *Citadel*, aimed at encircling the Soviet forces in the Kursk Salient. The strategic initiative on the Eastern Front now passes decisively to the Soviets
10	July	Allied forces land on Sicily
17	July	Beginning of the Soviet summer offensive
3	Sept.	Ceasefire between Italy and the Allied forces
5/6	Nov.	Soviets retake Kiev
28	Nov.–1 Dec.	Tehran Conference between Roosevelt, Stalin, and Churchill

1944

14–20	Jan.	Army Group North is driven back from Leningrad to Lake Peipus
6	June	Allied troops land in Normandy
22	June	Start of the great Soviet offensive against Army Group Centre. By July this entire German Army Group has been destroyed (losing around 400,000 men dead or captured)
20	July	July Bomb Plot to assassinate Hitler and instigate a military coup fails
1	Aug.–2 Oct.	Uprising of the Polish 'Home Army' (Armia Krajowa) in Warsaw
25	Aug.	Romania declares war on Germany
8	Sept.	Bulgaria declares war on Germany after Soviet troops march in
19	Sept.	Ceasefire between the USSR and Finland; Germans troops leave Finland
9–20	Oct.	Moscow Conference between Stalin, Churchill, and Harriman

1945

12	Jan.	Launch of a major Soviet offensive east of Warsaw
20	Jan.	Ceasefire between the USSR and the Hungarian opposition government
4–11	Feb.	Conference at Yalta in the Crimea between Stalin, Roosevelt, and Churchill
5	Apr.	Soviets renounce their April 1941 neutrality treaty with Japan
11	Apr.	Treaty of Friendship between the USSR and Yugoslavia under Marshal Tito
13	Apr.	Red Army takes Vienna
24–26	Apr.	June San Francisco Conference: Charter of the United Nations
25	Apr.	US and Soviet troops link up near Torgau on the River Elbe

30	Apr.	Hitler commits suicide in Berlin
7	May	Total surrender of the German *Wehrmacht* in Reims
9	May	The Germans repeat their total surrender at a signing ceremony in the Soviet HQ at Berlin–Karlshorst. End of the Second World War in Europe
17	July–2 Aug.	Potsdam Conference between Truman, Churchill (from 28 July replaced by Attlee), and Stalin
2	Sept.	Japanese surrender on board US battleship USS *Missouri* in Tokyo Bay. End of the Second World War

SUGGESTIONS FOR FURTHER READING

This list contains not only the newest major publications in the field. I have deliberately also included a number of older works whose significance I have come to appreciate in my research over the last few decades. A number of these works have never been translated into English, but are included as vital sources that will be of interest to anyone who can read German.

Armstrong, John A. (ed.), *Soviet Partisans in World War II* (Madison, WI, 1964).

Baberowski, Jörg, and Doering-Manteuffel, Anselm, *Ordnung durch Terror: Gewaltexzesse und Vernichtung im nationalsozialistischen und im stalinistischen Imperium* (2nd edn; Bonn, 2007).

Barber, John, and Harrison, Mark, *The Soviet Home Front 1941–1945: A Social and Economic History of the USSR in World War II* (London, 1991).

Böll, Heinrich, and Kopelew, Lew, *Warum haben wir aufeinander geschossen?* (Bornheim, 1981).

Burleigh, Michael, *The Third Reich: A New History* (London, 2000).

Chiari, Bernhard, *Alltag hinter der Front: Besatzung, Kollaboration und Widerstand in Weißrussland 1941–1944* (Düsseldorf, 1998).

Courtois, Stéphane, Bartosek, Karel, and Paczkowski, Adrzej, *The Black Book of Communism: Crimes, Terror, Repression* (Cambridge, 2004).

Creveld, Martin van, *Fighting Power: German and U.S. Army Performance, 1939–1945* (repr.; Westport, CT, 2007).

Dallin, Alexander, *German Rule in Russia: A Study of Occupation Policies* (London, 1957).

Dunn, Walter S., Jr., *The Soviet Economy and the Red Army, 1930–1945* (Westport, CT, 1995).

Èrenburg, Ilja, and Grossmann, Vassili S., *The Black Book: The Ruthless Murder of Jews by German–Fascist Invaders throughout the Temporarily Occupied Regions of the Soviet Union and in the Death Camps of Poland during the War of 1941–1945* (New York, 1981).

Erickson, John, *The Soviet High Command: A Military–Political History, 1918–1941* (London, 1962).

Erickson, John, *Stalin's War with Germany*, i. *The Road to Stalingrad* (London, 1975).

Erickson, John, *Stalin's War with Germany*, ii. *The Road to Berlin* (London, 1983).

Europa unterm Hakenkreuz. Die Okkupationspolitik des deutschen Faschismus (1938–1945), v. *Die faschistische Okkupationspolitik in den zeitweilig besetzten Gebieten der Sowjetunion (1941–1944)*, ed. and with an introduction by Norbert Müller et al. (Berlin, 1991).

Fritz, Stephen G., *Frontsoldaten: The German Soldier in World War II* (Lexington, KY, 1995).

Fritz, Stephen G., *Ostkrieg: Hitler's War of Extermination in the East* (Lexington, KY, 2011).

Gerlach, Christian, *Calculated Murders: German Economic Policies and the Politics of Annihilation in White Russia, 1941–1944* (Hamburg, 2000).

Germany and the Second World War, ed. Militärgeschichtliches Forschungsamt (Research Institute for Military History) (Potsdam, Germany; 8 vols; Oxford 1990–2008).

Glantz, David M., *Colossus Reborn: The Red Army at War, 1941–1943* (Lawrence, KS, 2005).

Glantz, David M., *Stumbling Colossus. The Red Army on the eve of World War* (Lawrence, KS, 2008).

Glantz, David M., *Operation Barbarossa: Hitler's Invasion of Russia 1941* (Brimscombe Port, 2011).

Glantz, David M., and House, Jonathan M., *When Titans Clashed: How the Red Army Stopped Hitler* (Lawrence, KS, 1995).

Hamburger Institut für Sozialforschung (ed.), *Verbrechen der Wehrmacht: Dimensionen des Vernichtungskrieges 1941–1944, Ausstellungskatalog* (Hamburg, 2002).

Hartmann, Christian, *Halder: Generalstabschef Hitlers 1938–1942* (2nd edn; Paderborn, 2009).

Hartmann, Christian, *Wehrmacht im Ostkrieg: Front und militärisches Hinterland 1941/42* (2nd edn; Munich, 2010).

Hartmann, Christian, Hürter, Johannes, Lieb, Peter, and Pohl, Dieter, *Der deutsche Krieg im Osten 1941–1944: Facetten einer Grenzüberschreitung* (Munich, 2009).

Herbert, Ulrich, *Hitler's Foreign Workers: Enforced Foreign Labour in Germany under the Third Reich* (Cambridge, 1997).

Hilberg, Raul, *The Destruction of the European Jews* (Chicago, 1961).

Hildermeier, Manfred, *Geschichte der Sowjetunion 1917–1991: Entstehung und Niedergang des ersten sozialistischen Staats* (Munich, 1998).

Hilger, Andreas, *Deutsche Kriegsgefangene in der Sowjetunion, 1941–1956: Kriegsgefangenenpolitik, Lageralltag und Erinnerung* (Essen, 2000).

Hillgruber, Andreas, *Hitlers Strategie: Politik und Kriegführung 1940–1941* (Frankfurt am Main, 1965; 3rd edn, 1993).

Hillgruber, Andreas, *Der Zweite Weltkrieg 1939–1945: Kriegsziele und Strategien der großen Mächte* (Stuttgart, 1982).

Hürter, Johannes, *Ein deutscher General an der Ostfront: Die Briefe und Tagebücher des Gotthard Heinrici 1941/42* (Erfurt, 2001).

Hürter, Johannes, *Hitlers Heerführer: Die deutschen Oberbefehlshaber im Krieg gegen die Sowjetunion 1941/42* (2nd edn; Munich, 2007).

Jackel, Eberhard, *Hitler's World View: A Blueprint for Power* (Cambridge, MA, 1981).

Jäger, Herbert, *Verbrechen unter Totalitärer Herrschaft. Studien zur nationalsozialistischen Gewaltkriminalität* (Olten, 1967).

Jarausch, Konrad H. (ed.), *Reluctant Accomplice: A Wehrmacht Soldier's Letters from the Eastern Front*, with contributions by Klaus J. Arnold and Eve M. Duffy and foreword by Richard Kohn (Princeton, 2011).

Kershaw, Ian, and Lewin, Moshe (eds), *Stalinism and Nazism. Dictatorships in Comparison* (Cambridge, 1997).

Kluge, Alexander, *Schlachtbeschreibung* (Olten, 1964).

Koenen, Gerd, *Der Russland-Komplex: Die Deutschen und der Osten 1900–1945* (Munich, 2005).

Krausnick, Helmut, and Wilhelm, Hans-Heinrich, *Die Truppe des Weltan-schauungskrieges. Die Einsatzgruppen der Sicherheitspolizei und des SD 1938–1942* (Stuttgart, 1981).

Krivosheev, Grigori F. (ed.), *Soviet Casualties and Combat Losses in the Twentieth Century* (London, 1997).

Kühne, Thomas, *Kameradschaft: Die Soldaten des nationalsozialistischen Krieges und das 20. Jahrhundert* (Göttingen, 2006).

Ledig, Gert, *The Stalin Front: A Novel of World War II* (New York, 2005).

Lexikon der Vertreibungen: Deportation, Zwangsaussiedlung und ethnische Säuberung im Europa des 20. Jahrhunderts, ed. Detlef Brandes, Holm Sundhausen, und Stefan Troebst (Vienna, 2010).

Lumans, Valdis O., *Himmler's Auxiliaries. The Volksdeutsche Mittelstelle and the German National Minorities of Europe 1939–1945* (Chapel Hill, NC, 1993).

Mawdsley, Evan, *Thunder in the East: The Nazi–Soviet War 1941–1945* (London, 2007).

Meier-Welcker, Hans, *Aufzeichnungen eines Generalstabsoffiziers 1939–1942* (Freiburg im Breisgau, 1982).

Megargee, Geoffrey P., *Inside Hitler's High Command* (Lawrence, KS, 2000).

Melvin, Mungo, *Manstein: Hitler's Greatest General* (London, 2010).

Merridale, Catherine, *Ivan's War: The Red Army, 1941–45* (London, 2005).

Müller, Rolf-Dieter (ed.), *Die deutsche Wirtschaftspolitik in den besetzten sowjetischen Gebieten 1941–1943. Der Abschlußbericht des Wirtschaftsstabes Ost und Aufzeichnungen eines Angehörigen des Wirtschaftskommandos Kiew* (Boppard am Rhein, 1991).

Müller, Rolf-Dieter, *Der letzte deutsche Krieg 1939–1945* (Stuttgart, 2005).

Müller, Rolf-Dieter, *The Unknown Eastern Front: The Wehrmacht and Hitler's Foreign Soldiers* (London, 2012).

Müller, Rolf-Dieter, and Ueberschär, Gerd R., *Hitler's War in the East 1941–1945: A Critical Assessment* (Providence, RI, 1997).

Musial, Bogdan, 'Konterrevolutionäre Elemente sind zu erschießen', in *Die Brutalisierung des deutsch–sowjetischen Krieges im Sommer 1941* (Berlin, 2000).

Musial, Bogdan (ed.), *Sowjetische Partisanen in Weißrussland: Innenansichten aus dem Gebiet Baranoviči 1941–1944. Eine Dokumentation* (Munich, 2004).

Neitzel, Sönke, *Tapping Hitler's Generals: Transcripts of Secrets Conversations, 1942–45* (Barnsley, 2007).

Oldenburg, Manfred, *Ideologie und militärisches Kalkül. Die Besatzungspolitik der Wehrmacht in der Sowjetunion 1942* (Cologne, 2004).

Osteuropa-Handbuch: Sowjetunion, Außenpolitik, i. *1917–1955*, ed. Dietrich Geyer (Cologne, 1972).

Otto, Reinhard, *Wehrmacht, Gestapo und sowjetische Kriegsgefangene im deutschen Reichsgebiet 1941/42* (Munich, 1998).

Overmans, Rüdiger, *Deutsche militärische Verluste im Zweiten Weltkrieg* (Munich, 1999).

Overy, Richard, *Russia's War* (London, 1998).

Philippi, Alfred, and Him, Ferdinand, *Der Feldzug gegen Sowjetrussland 1941 bis 1945: Ein operativer Überblick* (Stuttgart, 1962).

Pohl, Dieter, *Verfolgung und Massenmord in der NS-Zeit 1933–1945* (Darmstadt, 2003).

Pohl, Dieter, *Die Herrschaft der Wehrmacht: Deutsche Militärbesatzung und einheimische Bevölkerung in der Sowjetunion 1941–1944* (Munich, 2008).

Pospelov, P. N., et al. (eds), *Great Patriotic War of the Soviet Union, 1941–1945: A General Outline* (6 vols; Moscow, 1961).

Reese, Willy Peter, *A Stranger to Myself: The Inhumanity of War, 1941–44* (New York, 2005).

Reinhardt, Klaus, *Moscow—the Turning Point: The Failure of Hitler's Strategy in the Winter of 1941–42* (Oxford, 1992).

Rürup, Reinhard, and Jahn, Peter (eds), *Erobern und Vernichten: Der Krieg gegen die Sowjetunion 1941–1945. Essays* (Berlin, 1991).

Salisbury, Harrison E., *The 900 Days: The Siege of Leningrad* (Cambridge, 2003).

Schieder, Theodor, et al., *Documents on the Expulsion of the Germans from Eastern-Central Europa* (Bonn, 1960).

Schlögel, Karl, *Moscow, 1937* (Cambridge, 2012).

Schulte, Theo J., *The German Army and Nazi Policies in Occupied Russia* (Oxford, 1989).

Seaton, Albert, *The Russo-German War, 1941–45* (New York, 1971).

Shepherd, Ben, *War in the Wild East: The German Army and Soviet Partisans* (Cambridge, MA, 2004).

Shils, Edward, and Janowitz, Morris, 'Cohesion and Disintegration in the Wehrmacht', *Public Opinion Quarterly*, 12 (1948), S.280–315.

Snyder, Timothy, *Bloodlands: Europe between Hitler and Stalin* (New York, 2010).

Solzhenitsyn, Alexander, *Gulag Archipelago, 1918–1956. An Experiment in Literary Investigation* (3 vols; New York, 1974–8).

Streim, Alfred, *Die Behandlung sowjetischer Kriegsgefangener im 'Fall Barbarossa': Eine Dokumentation* (Heidelberg, 1981).

Streit, Christian, et al., *Die Wehrmacht und die sowjetischen Kriegsgefangenen 1941–1945* (3rd edn; Bonn, 1997).

Suny, Ronald Grigor, *The Soviet Experiment: Russia, the USSR and the Successor States* (New York, 1998).

Ueberschär, Gerd R., and Wette, Wolfram, 'Unternehmen Barbarossa', in *Der deutsche Überfall auf die Sowjetunion 1941: Berichte, Analysen, Dokumente* (Paderborn, 1984).

Die Verfolgung und Ermordung der europäischen Juden durch das nationalsozialistische Deutschland 1933–1945, vii. *Sowjetunion und annektierte Gebiete* I, compiled by Bert Hoppe (Munich, 2011).

Wegner, Bernd, *From Peace to War: Germany, Soviet Russia, and the World, 1939–1941* (Providence, RI, 1997).

Weinberg, Gerhard L., A World at Arms: A Global History of World War II (Cambridge, 1994).

Zellhuber, Andreas, 'Unsere Verwaltung treibt einer Katastrophe zu…', in *Das Reichsministerium für die besetzten Ostgebiete und die deutsche Besatzungsherrschaft in der Sowjetunion 1941–1945* (Munich, 2006).

PHOTOGRAPHIC ACKNOWLEDGEMENTS

INDEX

181